Marybeth's Final Journey

By: Ronda Rockwell

Copyright © 2013 Ronda Rockwell

All rights reserved. No part of this book may be reproduced in any form or by any electronic or mechanical means, including information storage and retrieval systems, without permission in writing from the publisher, except by a reviewer, who may quote brief passages in a review. Your support of the author's rights is appreciated.

Contact www.rondarockwellpublishing.com

Published by Ronda Rockwell Publishing

Printed by Createaspace, an Amazon Company

ISBN-13: 978-0-9896591-0-9

DEDICATION

This book is dedicated to my Mom, Marybeth.
Keep flicking the lights on and
sending the hummingbird.

CONTENTS

	Acknowledgments	i
	Introduction	3
1	Life Interrupted	Pg #7
2	The Diagnosis	Pg #26
3	Acceptance, Reflections and Wills	Pg #48
4	Hospice	Pg #67
5	The Signs	Pg #93
6	The Spiritual Journey	Pg #114
7	The Final Journey	Pg #125
8	The Last Goodbye	Pg #141
	Prologue	Pg #155

ACKNOWLEDGMENTS

Thank you Heather Hudson for encouraging me to share and write this book. Thank you to my family who gave me their blessings, Auntie M- Marti Gordon, Uncle J – John Hughes, Diana Martin, Michael Kaulbars and Crystal Kaulbars(Thanks Seestor for your editing help), to my children Brittney, Addie and Michael. Special Thanks to Marylou who helped make this book happen and thank you my husband Ron Rockwell for the love, comfort and the shoulder I needed while writing this.

Illustration Book Cover – Bojan and Ryan M

INTRODUCTION

   This incredible true story, Marybeth's Final Journey far different than any other book on the topic of living with cancer, coping with death, and the grieving process while encompassing spiritualism throughout the journey. This is a beautiful testimonial to the bond between my mother and myself. It is relatable and so very personal, that it will transport you along for the experience. This experience will take you on this journey that is full of love, humor, compassion, spiritual awakenings that will bring you to the brink of Heaven and open your eyes to the other side through a ghostly visit, and all of this is true and factual because I was there. My intention is to highlight life even while on knows they are dying from terminal cancer. To demonstrate how it is possible to face the inevitable with a smile. Each chapter you will share the entire process of living, working and raising a family until life smacks you in the face with an unexpected dose of reality, as it did for me, "Hey Ronda, your Mom is very sick and it's terminal cancer!"

   I was my Mom's daughter, her friend, and finally her caretaker at the time of her illness. There was no information to help me through this difficult time, to help my Mom, Marybeth, or myself. I hit the ground running and I learned as I went. There were no choices for me and by sharing my Mom's journey that is filled with lessons of coping through the myriad of emotions by the unknown medical hurdles and emotional obstacles that lay ahead. This shared experience is meant to give a whole new appreciation of life with your loved ones and to help find positive closures and strength to sustain the last goodbye.

   You may ask yourself, "Why is a story of terminal cancer incredible and why does it need to be shared?" There are millions of families facing their own similar events, approximately 11,000,000 people are diagnosed with cancer annually in the United States. Now multiply that by the family members, close friends and the caregivers touched by cancer. Each day approximately 1,500 people pass away from cancer in the United States. That is over one person every minute! Dying happens, yet it remains a mystery to all of us because it is considered a socially taboo subject in current American society. Our society as a whole finds this to be difficult subject despite being an inevitable and eventful fact.

When a death does occur, it's never at a perfect time in life where you are stress free from work or scheduled on vacation time, after the kids sports or dance lessons and after laundry is done for your family of five. Death is a very tough subject and without learning about it and sharing what a family feels and really goes when faced with a death of a close relative or friend, even a favorite celebrity, or a pet who'd been considered a family member. You will be taken off guard and no one is truly prepared for dying and grieving. It's overwhelming to say the least.

It's very easy to fall into the day in and day out routines of careers, raising a family, volunteer work, sports and all the assorted choices of living we all fill our time with. Some of us we may have very full, exciting lives and for others it may have a more relaxed flow. The younger we are the more invincible we feel, as if nothing could hurt us or stop us from anything. We tend to push the limits of life when we are young and we also haven't learned to appreciate of all the blessings we might have and often, as youths, we may take for granted our older family members.

Once we have had a chance to live, love, and grow older, that's when most of us finally appreciate life, every single day and every single moment. Our own mortality might finally be questioned, unlike our younger counterpart. Losing someone is never easy, especially if it is a young person. It makes it harder to rationalize their passing because they had so much yet to experience. When an elderly person passes, we are comforted in the fact that they had lived a long full life, and somehow we rationalize this as *okay*.

The events of this story had a purpose greater than I knew when I experienced them with my Mom and my family, and it is to share the real feelings, from happiness, sorrow, laughter and tears. I now have a much stronger belief in the spiritual other side of life. These events changed my life forever and oddly, in a positive way.

I've been blessed with a gift to overcome any challenge in life and find the good in situations that were far from being positive events. Life is not perfect and there are many circumstances that we don't have any choices in, as we go through the challenges. The choices we do have control of, are how we handle the hurdles life throws in front of us. We can always choose to learn from the things that occur in our lives, in our families, in friendships and at our jobs.

I had the blessings of my family to write and share this very private, intimate time in our family, for the simple hope that our experiences of losing a beloved family member to terminal cancer, will help the millions of other families just beginning this journey. This will be a very emotionally difficult time and hopefully I can help to bring a peace in life and death with love, courage and compassion.

Obviously, no two people are the same and no two journeys will be the same. Being an amateur researcher my whole life, this particular subject I had no information to draw from. I felt like I was just in a perpetual motion of accepting what needed to be done and doing it for my mom. There was no guide manual of what to expect or what will occur next.

It's with all my love and blessings that after you've shared Marybeth's Final Journey, for you too will find solace, peace, and a more positive way of handling the inevitable journey to lead to a higher quality of life instead of just passing on to the next one.

CHAPTER 1 - LIFE INTERRUPTED

In life, events can happen that will completely change the course of the road you are on and the direction you thought you were headed for with road blocks and curves, and can happen in a moment's notice. These can be so profoundly life altering it is almost an epiphany of one's soul and a wake-up call to live life more fully. In all beginnings there are endings, and with endings there are new beginnings; this is the true cycle of life. Just as in new life there will be death, that is a certainty. None of us can stop the final journey of dying. We don't know the hour, the day or the moment, but what is for certain, that one day we all will travel on our last road.

You or a loved one may be walking the final road of life now. For your impending loss, I grieve. I've felt and understand your pain, and believe my own account will help you cope through this by embracing your dying loved one much more closely so you can ensure they receive the love, dignity and quality of life you want to give them and will later reflect positively on, after they cross over. It's not just the loved one who has the illness that it affects, it becomes the entire family and friends' lives too. The not knowing what to expect, the fear of the illness, the fear of dying can be so overwhelming. My very dear friend, Heather, stuck by my side throughout Mom's journey from health to illness to the final inevitability. It was Heather's words of encouragement that drove me to share this utterly personal story with you and your family. I returned the favor when I stepped into the role of *listener* for Heather and her husband, Gary, who are, at the time of writing this book, facing similar circumstances of a terminally ill parent.

I'll share living, laughing, loving and dealing with the taboo subject of dying in a positive way. I hope that these words may bring some peace of the final journey for yourself or to your ill loved one. To help take away the fear that is associated with death and provide courage along the way.

We are born into a family and our first journey of life begins. As we grow and are nurtured by our moms, dads and grandparent if we're are so fortunate to have them. We may have other siblings or be the only child. We learn life skills that are taught by our families so that we can become happy, loving people when we grow up.

It's in this world, where life as we know it, is happening all around us, all the time. The living go through so many adventures, events, joys and walking on so many paths and experiencing many different journeys along the way. From infancy to adulthood we have lived, loved, laughed and cried providing all the memories we will reflect upon one day.

Reflecting of my own life and how different it was than most. It was not the traditional suburban family. So much happened to me, my siblings and to my Mom that movies could have been made of the things and events that occurred. After the age of 14, I didn't live with my Mom for a long time. Sporadic at most, and all for the things that happened, they just don't matter now. So very unimportant to where I am and to whom I am today or who my Mom became.

Somehow we survive being teenagers and young adults and as we mature, we marry and have our own families and careers. Then life becomes an endless array of errands after work, grocery shopping, laundry, housecleaning, running the kids to doctor appointments, countless birthday parties of their classmates and, pulling off magical holidays.

There are times in our lives where the most surreal events occur, which can cause our busy life to come to a screeching halt. These life changing events have such force to everything and everyone around, leaving you feeling breathless, as if all the air has been knocked out of your lungs. It's at this point in my life, this journey begins and life as I knew it, as my Mom knew it, would forever change and become life interrupted.

My Mom was born July 16, 1940, Mary Elizabeth Hughes, in San Diego, Ca. She was fondly called Marybeth by her friends and her parents. Her parents were Vernon and Pauline Hughes. She was the oldest of three children. She has a younger sister Martha Melody and a brother John David. Her upbringing was having that 1950's nuclear family ideal. She went graduated Hoover High School.

Marybeth was always a beauty. She was tall, 5' 10" and stunning. Beautiful brown eyes that sparkled when she spoke and a smile that was so warm. Her laugh would tickle your ears to hear. She was born with dark hair like my Papa's, her father. Over the years she wore her hair blond, strawberry blonde or a chestnut brown, depending on her mood, and she was *always* impeccably dressed. She had so much style and flair.

As a woman, during the time she grew up, you graduated school, went to college, married and had children. This was her future or at least what American culture dictated at the time. Somewhere along the way, during the women's movement, my sweet Mom found out she had more choices in life, one of the choices was a need to be happy and loved in the right marriage. She tried to find the fairytale-kind-of-love her parents shared. Needless to say, her final husband, was not a good fit, to say it mildly. My Mom had been living on the East Coast with her 5th husband (yes her 5th) and she wasn't happy. During a phone conversation, she told me she was going to divorce him and I offered for her to come stay with my family, to come back home to San Diego.

That was 11 years ago and she remained living with my family always. She shared as my three kids grew up, Brittney, Addie and Michael. As I had three grandchildren, Jake, Joshua and Brendon, she had three more great-grandchildren. She had twelve grandchildren and seventeen great grandchildren! She lived with me through my divorce and my new marriage. My Mom shared life with me, as I shared life with her. It was a mutual choice. she doted on all her grandkids, great-grandkids and called at least once a month to all of us to stay in close touch with the giant family she'd created. She was really the glue that held much together. Her dynamic charisma was a force to be reckoned with, always.

Marybeth was a very intelligent woman. She was very fortunate in that she actually landed the job she had in her annual from Lincoln High School – she mentioned that her dream job was becoming a Medical Receptionist and that's just what she was for a period in her life. She was a hub of communication, a wonderful positive calm in many stormy seas. She rarely raised her voice or showed any anger, but when she did she could raise Hell itself. I liken it to quiet thunder and classy at that because she had her moments of ire. She worked in the medical field for a good portion of her working career and in the late 1980'she became successful business owner with three successful hair salons in San Diego, called Screamin' Scissors. She taught educational classes, was involved in multiple Organizations. She was such a natural people person and could engage conversations where ever she went.

Mom worked until she was 69, up until she had a major stroke, and finally retired. I always said she had angels looking out after her, because she was blessed with all of her functions after the stroke, even the doctors were amazed and happy how well she was doing considering what could have been the alternative. The only thing that was more apparent and I noticed was that she tired easy and took more naps. As she rested more, I had no idea it was not from being older and not the after effects of the stroke.

Life continued with the forward motion. When I couldn't take the time off work for the doctor appointments for Mom, my husband Ron would take her. My Mom went to a doctor appointment at least monthly now. Our new family was working well together, sharing a loving, happy home. It was just my sixteen year old son, Michael, my Mom and my new husband Ron and I living together. My middle daughter Addie and her three year old son had just recently moved out.

Life had a nice calm to it and my Mom had said, "Now we can enjoy some adult time". In the middle of the brief peace, *pow*! My husband received a phone call from his sister Sheri in New York, their dad had just passed away from a stroke. My heart was broken for him, for his sister Sheri and his brother Scott. Death is something we all know will happen to each of us one day. There is *never* a good time to go and for most we don't know when that will be.

Mom and Michael stayed in San Diego, while we spent a week in New York. Bittersweet for my husband, as he missed his whole family, and this was definitely not a vacation, but allowed him to see all of his family. It was in March when we arrived and typically in upstate New York there would have feet of snow, as my husband told me. It was very cold but no snow.

We stayed at his parent's home in Ticonderoga. Scott, Ron's brother, came to stay at the house as well. Ron's sister Sheri, lived very close, so the brothers and sister could visit, hug, cry and grieve together. The night before the service Ron and I met Sheri and her kids at the Firehouse Hall to set up tables and chairs and decorate with the photographs and flowers. We got everything ready in preparation for tomorrow. That evening we returned back to Ron's parent's home and we all shared a lovely dinner and conversations together.

The next morning we woke up to snow and it was breathtaking. Being raised a *beach girl* in San Diego; the snow was exciting to see. The sun glistened on the white blanket of snow that covered every tree and the entire ground. I ran outside in my pajamas and slippers like a little girl on Christmas morning, to go frolic in the snow. Ron and his family laughed at me in my enthusiasm of the cold, white wonder. I scooped up two handfuls of snow, made a snowball and threw it at my husband! Of course he gladly returned the love and threw one back. His brother Scott joined us too. We laughed some more after our impromptu snow ball fight and then had to go get ready for the service for their dad Vernie.

It was a surreal day for the service and the snow made such a statement. I was there supporting my husband and his family emotionally and love. It was a beautiful day for a celebration of life for his dad. The service was held at the Firehouse Hall in Ticonderoga. Sheri played music before the services that she lovingly picked out, and when the family and friends arrived there was a lovely prayer service for Vernie. After the service ended everyone stayed and had a luncheon together. We returned to my Sharon and Francis' home, mother and father-in-law. Everyone visited, sharing stories of life. It was an emotional evening too. Saying goodbye to a loved one that has passed on is never easy, especially when it's a parent.

The next morning we had to fly home to San Diego. My sister-in-law, Sheri, two of her boys and Ron's mom, Sharon drove us the two hour trip from Ticonderoga to the Albany Airport. We all had our tearful hugs and goodbyes, then went through security and boarded our plane back to the West Coast. We returned to San Diego International Airport late that evening and we were very happy to get home. I missed my family. I missed our home. My oldest daughter, Britt, picked us up that evening. When we arrived home it was late, so I didn't want to wake up my Mom and I let her sleep. My son Michael gave me a big hug. I was so happy to see him. We visited briefly and then we all went to bed out of emotional exhaustion and tomorrow was back to the routine of life.

Up at 5:00 a.m. every morning to get ready for work, to arrive at my office about 6:15 a.m. I never could say good morning to my Mom anymore, since she retired. Lucky woman, she was able to sleep in. I worked all day, as did my husband and I would get home about 4:00pm every afternoon. On a typical weekday, my Mom would be sitting in the patio on her favorite wrought iron chair under the light blue table umbrella. She would be drinking a cup of coffee and smoking a cigarette, and she would always look up at me and ask with a big smile,

"Hi honey how was your day?"

My response would be typically the same, "Hi Mama, another busy day."

Simple, but oh so comforting and very easy to take for granted. Like the night sky falling or the morning sun rising. I would sit and drink a cup of coffee with her and my husband, out on the patio. Mom especially liked being outside on the patio, with the beautiful blue skies and golden sunsets. She would refer to our patio as *'the secret garden'*. We would visit for a bit, before Ron was off to his second job. Our usual routine was having a quick dinner together, then Mom would lie down and watch T.V. in her room or play games on social media, before finally drifting off to sleep later. The afternoon after Ron and I returned from New York was very different, Mom wasn't herself. There was no usual greeting, no smile or the familiar question, *'Hi Honey, how was your day?'* She wasn't on the patio having her usual cup of coffee and that *was* odd. She'd been an avid coffee drinker years before I was born. In fact, We used to joke that if she could, she'd have an I.V. of coffee hooked up to her at all times. When I'd say that, she'd laugh and say, *'Yes, I would'*. She really loved her coffee that much, which is why I was alarmed that she wasn't up that afternoon having a cup.

When she wasn't up that first afternoon that we were back from New York, I just thought *"She must be extra tired?"* She didn't get up for dinner right way either. When she finally emerged from her bedroom, she looked tired and I asked her if she was okay. She answered in her most reassuring voice, "Yes sweetie, I'm okay, just tired." I had the distinct feeling she wasn't being completely honest with me, and most importantly, herself.

Later that evening, I was putting the leftovers away in the refrigerator, and that's when I noticed all of the fresh vegetables and food didn't seemed to be touched, that we had bought before leaving for New York. I had made sure to buy easy things for my Mom and Michael to prepare. At the time, I didn't think much of it, except maybe they went out to dinner a lot.

The next afternoon when I arrived at home from work, Mom was still laying down. She didn't get up right away when dinner was ready and later when she finally woke up, she ate a light dinner, took her medicines and said she was just really tired and was going back to bed. I gave her a hug and said goodnight to her. I was getting a little worried and nervous. When Mom had her stroke, I actually had just come home from being in the hospital myself, for a couple nights for my heart. I always felt I had worried Mom into the stroke, even though she smoked for 50 years and had coronary artery disease.

Remembering the night of her stroke, she didn't seem well and I said we need to go have her checked out. Dinner had just come out of the oven and she said, "If I have to go to the hospital I am going to eat dinner first!" I pleaded for her to go now, but she was stubborn. She sat down and ate dinner, then went and changed into aqua blue jeans, a matching top and her jewelry. She finally *allowed* us to take her up to the Urgent Care and was transferred immediately to the Stroke Ward of the hospital for five nights! We all had a good laugh about it afterwards, including Mom. Her vanity required her to be dressed well!

Wednesday went okay and Mom was having coffee when I got home from work, so in my head I thought, *"Oh good. She's feeling better because she is drinking her coffee"*. We actually were able to have a nice visit. I felt like I hadn't seen her in almost two weeks. Thursday after work was far different, this was the day life was interrupted from anything I would ever know. It started out like a typical workday. I woke up, got showered, made coffee and woke up Ron. I got ready and woke up Michael for school. Then I left for work at the office.

    I looked forward to Thursdays, because Ron had the evening off his second job and we would have a nice family dinner together. Ron had planned to BBQ some New York steaks, this was one of my Mom's favorites and we only had it once in a blue moon and if it was on sale. He also was making his homemade mac-n-cheese, another one of Mom's favorites.

    Mom was still laying down when I arrived home from work that evening. I walked into the kitchen and Ron was a busy chef preparing dinner. I hugged and kissed him and asked if Mom had been up at all?

He said "She just got up for a drink." I knocked on her door and said,

"Mama, can I come in?"

"Yes sweetie, come in."

I opened her door and walked into her room toward her bed. She looked really tired. I asked her if she ate that day and she said she had a cup of soup. I told her about the yummy special dinner Ron was cooking because he knew she would love it. She smiled and said, "Yummy. I'll be up soon."

    I walked out onto the patio, motion my hand to Ron to follow me outside and softly asked, so she wouldn't hear me say "I think something might be wrong with her. She just didn't seem like herself and she seems so tired. I'm getting worried". Ron agreed with me and we both thought we may need to take her into Urgent Care. Dinner was ready and I went to let Mom and Michael know. Ron served us all dinner. Mom sat at the dining room table and I remember quite clearly, watching her ease down in the chair and hold her right side, by her ribs. She winced. I immediately asked her

"Mama, are you okay?"

"Well my ribs feel so soar, it really has hurt the last couple days".

I was nervous now. Mom *never* complained about *anything*. She had shingles about four years ago and it started with the same feeling on one side of her ribs and she had a small rash then. I asked her if she had a rash now, like from the shingles. She said no.

I kept an eye on Mom for about a minute, if that. She wasn't eating at all and she was holding her side. Worried of her heart condition, stroke or shingles coming again, I said, "Mama, I would like to take you up to the Urgent Care to get examined and make sure you are okay?" This time around, she didn't say *"Wait until I eat my dinner"* and she didn't get dressed up. She just said okay let's go. I *knew* something was wrong. Michael stayed back at the house and he was going to put dinner away while we had a doctor check her out. Ron helped Mom into the front seat of my FJ Cruiser, he hopped in back and away we went. This trip to the hospital would prove to be far different than from any other before.

The first Urgent Care we went to by our hospital was no longer part of our plan with our family doctor, but referred us to a new Urgent Care. I was a bit upset that they wouldn't even do vitals on Mom. This is when I was upset about the healthcare system we have in America, however, I kept my opinions to myself, and I went back to my concern of my Mom. So we walked to get the FJ and away we went to try to find the other Urgent Care. I am grateful this happened. The new Urgent Care closed at 8:00pm and it was about 7:40pm when we arrived. There were only two other patients in the lobby. I explained my Mom's current condition and her past medical issues.

They took her right back for triage. When the doctor came in, he was an older man and his demeanor was very compassionate. We explained her symptoms and I said that I didn't think she has eaten for a while. I told him about all the food that was not touched the week before, when we were in New York, and I was concerned because she is sleeping so much more than normal and she was having pain in her ribs and I gave him a quick synopsis of her medical history.

During the exam, Mom was coughing so he ordered a chest x-ray and some labs while we waited in the room with her. She had the x-ray's and blood drawn and we waited. We were the last people in the Urgent Care and I could hear the doctor on the phone consulting another doctor and realized it was about Mom. He came in and explained what he thinks is going on in her lungs. That he cannot say for certain from the x-ray what it is but there is a large mass in her left lung and looks infused. He said, " It could just be fluid on the lungs, but either way she would need to go to the hospital." He continued speaking,

"I am not an admitting doctor or I would admit her now." I asked him,

"Can we take her home until the morning and then ask her doctor to admit her so such doesn't have to suffer and wait all night in the ER?"

"Yes, I would have to agree with you. There is no reason she should have to be subjected and exposed to all the illness of the ER."

The doctor and I both agreed that if she could be there all night while tests are run. He was fine with us taking care of her at home and he prescribed pain medication for her. He also was going to write a detailed report and fax it to her doctor's office now and when her doctor reads this report he will admit her right away. He gave us a copy of his findings and her prescriptions. We thanked him for all of his help.

I told Mom that I was sorry she was sick, but we would find out whatever it is and get her well. As we drove back down to our neighborhood, my mind was racing of *"the large mass"* in her lung. Those words echoed in my head. I'm sure she was thinking the same thing. I had to remind myself the doctor *did* say it could just be fluid, so I tried very hard to not worry yet or let Mom see I was worried. I had to wear my poker face. We filled her medicines, drove home and got her tucked in bed.

I told her that I would call her doctor at 9:00am when the office opened and would give her a call about going up to the hospital. I gave her a kiss good night and hugged her. I told her that the doctors would make her better. I was doing my best to be cheerful and loving, when inside I was scared of the possibilities.

I remember walking upstairs with my husband and as we got changed into our pajamas and discussed my worries of the big "*C*" word. Cancer. I didn't want to say that horrible, ugly word out loud. As much as it was possible for there to be just a mass of fluid, there was a possibility of it being lung cancer. We climbed into bed and kissed goodnight. I could barely sleep out of worry for my Mom. Just when I finally fell asleep, my alarm went off blaring in my ear.

I got up and showered and proceeded to get ready for work. I also made sure I was dressed comfortable, as we would be in the hospital and I didn't know what to expect or how long my Mom would be in there. My husband and son got ready for the day as well. I knocked gently on my Mom's door and walked in. I wanted to make sure she took her pain medicine and to see if she needed anything. She sleepily smiled at me and said she would just sleep until I called.

Off to work I went on that Friday morning which simply felt like a continuation of Thursday from the lack of sleep. I told my supervisor what happened last night and that my Mom would be admitted to the hospital today. He was very nice and said to do what I needed to do. I made sure I took care of any urgent business matters and watched the clock. I took a break at 9:00am so I could call the doctor's office. I spoke to the receptionist and explained what happened last night and there should be a fax from the Urgent Care doctor.

She said, "Yes they had received it." She asked me a few questions about my Mom's health status and asked if she could put me on hold? The doctor picked up the phone and he asked me a few more questions and said they would make the arrangements for admission to the hospital and the hospital would call me once they had a room ready. Let me tell you, this felt like a very long wait, however, they called me back in thirty minutes to tell me to bring her in and check in at the main hospital entrance at the admissions office.

I called Mom's cell phone and she answered. I calmly told her that her doctor had made her arrangements and that there is a five star room ready at the hospital. I also told her I would be home in about ten minutes. Thankfully, I live about five to ten minutes from my office. I checked out of work, turned my computer off and drove home. I got her loaded in the car and we headed up to the hospital. She was dressed in her pajamas and her little white corduroy cap.

I knew she didn't feel good, because for my entire life my Mom *always* dressed to the nines. Her hair, her makeup, her clothes, shoes and jewelry all had to look good. As a teenager she was called "Ms. Revlon", wearing her deep red lipstick and looking picture perfect. She had raised me, my two sisters and brother to always look nice too. On holidays, even if we were staying in, we dressed for the occasion. So today, her leaving the house in her pajamas with no makeup, I knew she was not feeling well. She was wearing her white corduroy hat though.

As we drove on the freeway towards the hospital, I said to Mom, "I'm so sorry you are sick and that you have to go through testing. I love you and just want you better. Also, my supervisor was so nice and he said go do what I needed to do". I knew she would be worried about my job (because I would worry), and I absolutely didn't want her to be concerned with me. This was all about her and getting her on the mend.

She said, "Honey, I love you too and I want to feel better". The hospital was about fifteen minutes away. When we arrived, I drove to the front entrance to get a wheelchair for her and one of the hospital attendants came out to help me get my Mom wheeled inside, while I parked the car. I parked in the parking garage and hurried up to Mom.

We got her registered and a nurse came down to wheel her to her room. Up the elevator we went and arrived on the third floor. The nurse wheeled her down the hall into her room and had her dress into a hospital gown. I assisted Mom with dressing and tied up the gown. I helped her get the hospital no slip socks on her feet and Mom grabbed her little white cap and put it back on her head. She smiled and said, "I didn't have time to color my hair and my gray roots are showing." We both laughed at her vanity.

Having made more hospital trips for illness, surgeries, children's births and grandchildren's births, I knew this patient area did not allow for overnight guests. She had a private room, with no view, a small private restroom and one sitting chair. She had a similar room when she was on the Stroke Ward, and overnight guests were not allowed there, due to the severity of illness. This alarmed me a bit. *If it's just fluid on her lung, why can't I stay?* I thought to myself.

Her nurse hooked up her IV and soon the plethora of testing would begin. I texted my family her room number and her direct phone number for the hospital room. I let everyone know that I will text once we know anything. So we waited for the doctor to come in for assessment and for a direction of all the tests to be conducted. He ordered a CT Scan and some preliminary blood tests. He explained what Pleural Effusion was, as noted on the information from the Urgent Care doctor's notes and wanted a look at her lungs. It is excess fluid that is between two layers and can fill the space that surrounds the lungs and can make breathing more difficult.

So as we both waited in her room, she just wanted to sleep. There is something about hospitals that zaps my energy and I get so sleepy. Maybe it's because being in the hospital, other than a Mom giving birth is not usually a happy event. The emotional stress both the patient and the family feel can be overwhelming at times. There are even some people who refuse to go into a hospital either of fear of being around sick people or that their only hospital experience was not a good one, so they just simply stay away, from the emotional fear.

Mom had to have so many different blood tests and one of them was to draw blood every ten minutes to get a certain read of her blood cells. I couldn't keep track of all the names of tests being performed. She was already frail and her skin so thin. In the last four months her skin had begun getting these large dark purple blotches on them, mostly around her hands and forearms. When we had asked her regular doctor about them we were simply told it's because she is on certain blood thinners. This seemed like a reasonable explanation at the time.

I stayed with her all day and into the evening as she went through her assorted tests. By the end of this evening, there was no conclusive result as to what this was. I spoke to her nurse and asked if there were more tests for the evening and she said she didn't see anything scheduled, but they were still waiting for the pulmonologist specialist to come in and he may schedule more tests for tomorrow. I wrote my cell phone number on the small white board in Mom's hospital room and asked the nurse to have the doctor call me if he knew of anything.

It was near the end of visiting hours, so I gave Mom a hug and kiss and told her I would be up early in the morning and bring her real coffee. She smiled and said, "Okay Honey. I love you and I will just rest. I will be alright." Even in her illness the mom in her was trying to comfort *me*, her daughter. I told her I would record our ghost shows too. That made her smile. Friday night was our night to get into our pajamas, grab our comforters and sit together getting scared about the ghosts not at rest. We enjoyed this together.

    I drove home, set record on the DVR and collapsed in my bed. The next morning I showered and got dressed in comfortable clothes and tennis shoes, as I had a feeling we would be all over the hospital for more tests and procedures. I made coffee, drank a cup and then filled a travel coffee cup for Mom. I talked with my husband and asked him if he would bring up Michael to come see Grandma later, and he said yes. I told him I would call when I knew what schedule of tests would be happening. My husband gave me such a big hug and told me it would be alright. I kissed him goodbye and drove back to the hospital on auto-pilot.

    When I arrived to my Mom's hospital room, her day nurse was in the room. I asked her if there were any results back. She let me know the pulmonologist had ordered a Thoracentesis. I asked what that was and she explained it's a procedure where they extract fluid that has built up around the lungs. A long needle is used to extract the fluid, the patient is awake and a local anesthetic is used so they won't feel any pain, maybe just some pressure.

    She explained that the procedure is performed in Radiology and they are trying to get my Mom scheduled. Due to the procedure there will be a small team of people to assist in the procedure. I later found out that the danger of this *simple* procedure is that the lung could collapse, so the medical team needs to be ready, should anything go wrong. I was relieved to hear it was fluid in her lung instead of a tumor from cancer. I gave Mom a hug and she told me about her night. She said,

"Just when I would fall asleep, they would come in and take me for a scan or come in and draw my blood or take my blood pressure. I am so tired."

" Mama I am so sorry that you had to be a pin cushion, but at least we are finding out what is wrong."

I asked her if she was in pain and she said she was. I called her nurse for pain medicine for her and quietly explained outside of her room, to her nurse, that they would need to ask her if she was in pain, as she may not admit it unless asked directly. She's such a strong woman and would never complain, *never*. The nurse gave her some pain medicine and as it began taking effect, you could see some relief on Mom's face.

Through the course of the day, Mom received some phone calls from family. Ron and Michael stopped in to see Grandma later in the day. When they came for a visit, I excused myself for a quick break. I called my daughter Britt. She was making baby-sitting arrangements for her kids and she would be on her way up to see Grandma too.

My husband and son left for home and soon my daughter Britt arrived. She gave Grandma a big hug and kiss. She visited for a couple hours with us and said she would come back soon to visit. After Britt left, Mom and I waited for the Thoracentesis. It was scheduled for the late afternoon downstairs in Radiology. A technician walked into my Mom's room with a wheelchair and said that they were ready for her. I reassured Mom she would be okay and she wouldn't hurt from this. I knew she was scared.

We walked to the elevator as my Mom was pushed in the wheelchair. We loaded into the elevator and pushed the button for the basement level. The tech wheeled my Mom to the check-in counter of Radiology. She was the last patient of the afternoon. After her check-in I kissed her and said,

"I will be waiting for you. You will be okay. I love you", and smiled at her.

"I love you too." She smiled back.

I sat alone in this large waiting area. Nervously waiting and praying my Mom would be okay. Once in a while a doctor or nurse would walk past in the hallway. About an hour had passed and just about the time my Mom should be brought out, there was this God-awful screaming or moaning coming from the direction of the procedure rooms. I had never heard anything like this unearthly moaning sound in my life. There was no one walking in the hallway.

The moaning was so loud I was just getting up to see if someone needed help. It was at that moment that a doctor and a technician were walking towards each other, opposite in the hallway, and the tech asked

"What is that sound?", the doctor replied,

"That's our ghost down here. You haven't heard about our moaning ghost in the wall? We don't know who he was, but he is here and is loud."

The doctor and technician continued walking and the moaning finally stopped. So, now I am a little creeped out, alone again and thinking, *"Great. I get to be alone with the moaning hospital ghost!"*

About five minutes later the radiologist tech wheeled my Mom out and we returned upstairs to her room. I asked my Mom if she was okay, and she said yes. Her nurse came in the room to help get her settled and let her know that for about the next 24 hours she would need to practice breathing deep breaths. There had been so much fluid on her lungs that had created a lot of pressure. She also mentioned that the fluid would be tested too. Her nurse asked her how her pain was and she said she's hurting. She was given more pain medicine.

My Mom rested and I visited with her. I told her about the moaning ghost in the hallway downstairs. We had a laugh about that. Her dinner came and I helped her get comfortable. She ate very little. I figured with what she had to go through today, made her lose her appetite. I got her comfortable and asked if she wanted to watch TV; she said no she just wants to sleep. I gave her a hug and kiss and said to have sweet dreams and I would be back up first thing in the morning. She smiled and said she loved me.

As I walked to my car, I felt relief come over me. I was thinking how lucky she was and I was so thankful she had no complications from the procedure. I wished I could have spent the night with her but hopefully she would come home tomorrow afternoon. I drove home completely exhausted both emotionally and physically. The stress had caught up to me with what my sweet Mom was going through. It did not matter what I needed to do for her. I would do anything I had to.

CHAPTER 2 - THE DIAGNOSIS

Sunday Morning I woke thinking "*Okay. Today I can bring Mama home*". I showered, drank a cup of coffee and made a travel cup of coffee for my Mom. Ron said he would make her bed and get her laundry done. He wanted to make sure it was nice when she came home. I gave him a hug and kiss and told him I would let him when we would be home.

I drove to the hospital and entered the parking garage. I laughed to myself . "*I really need my own hospital parking space for as many times as I come to the hospital*." I parked and hurriedly walked into the main entrance of the hospital towards the elevators. It seemed to take forever for the elevator to get to the lobby floor, but it soon arrived and dinged. I rode up to the third floor and walked toward Mom's room, stopping by the nurse station.

I asked, "Who is my Mom, Marybeth's day nurse and is she available to speak with?" The nurse at the reception counter said she would send her down when she was done with her other patient. I thanked her and walked into my Mom's room. She was up and just finished a light breakfast. I said,

"Hi Mama. I brought you real coffee." Her eyes lit up and she thanked me and said,

"Oh good some real coffee!" We both laughed.

I asked her if she had been told anything from the doctors or nurses yet. She said no not yet. As we visited and she told me about last night I noticed she was using oxygen now. She said that she had another x-ray of her chest too. Soon, her day nurse came in and introduced herself. We shook hands and I asked her if there were any results back yet and she explained that they are still waiting on some to come in but that the pulmonologist had ordered an Endoscopy of her lungs to check things out. This seemed reasonable to me but I still had questions about why. I asked the nurse if she knew when the pulmonologist doctor would be in, and she didn't know? The hospital staff, were doing a very good job of caring for my Mom and they were keeping her pain free. This led to some funny conversations with her a bit loopy from the medicine.

Later in the day both of my daughters came by to see Grandma and they brought their three children, Jake, Joshua and Brendon. My grandsons called my Mom *Oma* and they loved her so much! When the kids arrived, she smiled so big. Her eyes twinkled seeing her great grandbabies and they brought her such joy and happiness. Each of the little ones climbed onto the hospital bed to give Oma a hug and kiss and then they sat with her for a visit. We all took some pictures of them together.

My daughters asked if we had any results back yet and I said, "No, but I keep asking. They were going to schedule an Endoscopy sometime tomorrow." My family had been through this procedure with me for other reasons. An Endoscopy is a camera the doctors will sometimes use to look inside of your body without a surgery. The patient is put in a twilight sleep, so they don't have to know that a tube is inserted in their mouth and a tiny camera is inserted to give a real time view internally. The procedure takes about an hour with set up and the test itself. An anesthesiologist is there along with the doctor, nurse and technicians.

I could see that Mom was getting tired, so I let my kids know Grandma needed to take a nap soon. They all said their goodbyes and each of the little ones gave Oma a kiss. Britt asked me to call her if I heard anything back. I assured her I would. She also wanted to know when Grandma's test was scheduled because she wanted to be here for Grandma and to be with me tomorrow.

After they left, I dozed off for a little bit in the chair, as my Mom napped. Her nurse would come in periodically to check her vitals, which would wake us up. Each time the nurse came in, I would ask about the results on her blood work? She said she would check and see. Our whole family seemed to be in the dark as to why she had the fluid on her lungs. I was so thankful that was all it was, but we still wanted to know why.

By the end of the day the nurse came in to let us know that they were still trying to get a time scheduled for tomorrow, however, it being Sunday evening, they probably would not be able to give a time until tomorrow on Monday morning when Radiology reopened. Mom was responding well to the antibiotics and her pain was managed, which was a relief for her and me. It was so hard to watch my Mom go through all this. She wanted to come home as much as I wanted to take her home.

Her dinner tray came in and I got her settled to eat. She said that she would be okay and suggested that I should go get some rest too. Inside I really agreed with her. Between my diabetes and fibromyalgia, the stress of my Mom's illness was taking a toll on my mind and body. But anything I was going through, was *nothing* compared to what she was. I would do anything for her and I didn't want to leave, nor did I want her to worry about me.

So I smiled at her and said, "Okay Mama. You are probably right. I will call the nurse first thing in the morning and I will be here before they take you for your Endoscopy. If the doctor happens to come in, please have him call me." I gave her a hug and kiss then I stopped by the nurses' station to ask her nurse to please leave a note for the morning nurse to call me on my cell phone or my office number when the Endoscopy was scheduled. I needed to be here for my Mom and would drive up before the tests would start. She assured me that I would be contacted before the procedure would take place. I thanked her and left.

I walked down to the parking garage and sat a moment in my car to collect myself. Having to see my Mom go through all these tests and not being able to spend the nights with her was taking an emotional toll on me as well as a physical one. I summoned up the energy to drive, turned the car on and drove home. I was so tired from the last four days of the hospital. All I wanted was for Mom to be okay and come home. I arrived home, parked and walked inside the house. I immediately hugged my husband and son. My husband was so sweet and he had dinner waiting for me, which was so nice. I ate dinner and then went upstairs, took a shower to wash the hospital off.

I hoped into bed, kissed my husband goodnight and fell asleep. I slept a little better than I had been sleeping; knowing Mom was on the mend. I needed to be fresh for work tomorrow. Timing of life's challenges seems to sometimes happen all at once. The art of multi-tasking career, family and emotions are something I am good at doing. However, at my office, they would be changing the accounting software and training us in the week ahead. I needed to be extra focused at work and also available to care for my sweet mama.

The alarm blared in my ear. I jumped up and started my typical routine. I went into the office the and spoke to my supervisor to apprise him of the procedure my Mom would need to have today and I asked to leave when the hospital called. He said "Yes, of course." It was about 10:00 a.m. when I finally received the call from the hospital and the Endoscopy was scheduled at 11:00 am. I immediately called my daughter Britt and told her I was headed up to the hospital now, she said she would meet me up there. I then called my Mom and told her I was on my way up, in the best cheerful voice I could manage.

I knew she was scared and I wanted to keep her calm and simply love her with my support. I was on auto pilot as I drove to the hospital from my office. I parked in the hospital parking garage and quickly made it into the hospital, down to the elevator and up to her room. I gave her a big hug and kiss when I walked in. I could see in her face she was happy and relieved I was there. I told her Britt was going to come up for more support. She smiled. We had a nice visit talking about life, the grandkids, real coffee and taking her home soon.

I understood how tired being a patient in a hospital was. Just as you finally fall asleep the nurse would come in for vitals or you had to go through more blood tests and it began to make you feel like an exhausted pin cushion. Brittney arrived just as the technician came to Mom's room with a wheelchair to take her downstairs for the procedure. Britt and I walked behind her as the technician led us to a special elevator for patients only. The Endoscopy was to be performed downstairs in the Radiology area. We were allowed to wait with Mom as the technicians prepared everything ready for the doctor. I held her hand and tried to comfort her.

When the pulmonologist doctor arrived he explained to all of us what he would do during the procedure and then asked us to wait in the private waiting room down the hall. I gave Mom a kiss on the cheek and let her know we would see her soon. We walked to the waiting room. This was smaller than the one I was in during her Thorentisus and the moaning ghost. There were a few other patients waiting for their procedures and some family members that were waiting for their loved ones tests to be done. There were about ten chairs lining the walls of the room, a table with old magazines, and a TV. We sat there clock watching and not really saying too much. I prayed for my Mom in my quite thoughts. About forty-five minutes had passed and the doctor came to the waiting room to talk to me and Britt.

He asked us to please follow him. We walked down the hallway and he opened a door that was marked *Private Consultation*. This room was almost directly across from the procedure rooms. The room was small decorated with a few chairs and a little table that had a box of Kleenex. He gestured with his hands, for us to please sit down, as he stood leaning against the white wall, in his hospital green surgical scrubs. I was thinking he was just going to let us know why she had fluid on her lung and to tell us she would be going home.

Brittney and I sat down. The doctor had a very somber look on his face and he began telling us that after he had performed the Thorentisus on Saturday and removed the fluid that had built up around her lungs, he ordered another x-ray which confirmed a large mass remaining in her left lung. The reason for the Endoscopy was to get a better look at the mass, inside of her lung. Very gently he said that he has ordered a biopsy of the tissue samples of the mass, that will take one to two days for confirmation of cancer, but he is certain it is cancer. He said in all of his years of being a doctor, he couldn't be more certain even without the biopsy confirmation. A cancerous tumor has a very distinct look.

The room suddenly got smaller and my brain almost couldn't process what he was saying. "*Cancer? Did he just say Cancer? Oh no!*", I thought. "*No!*" And then it hit me. I couldn't breathe, I couldn't move and the tears flowed down my face. "*My Mom just had fluid on her lungs. No one told me she still had a mass in her lung? This just can't be cancer!*" I thought. Then the realization hit and it felt like this was a bad movie scene when the doctor comes to speak with the family waiting for the surgery to be over and the doctor has to tell the family their loved one didn't make it. How cliché, but *this* doctor had just told me *my* Mom has lung cancer! This is not a movie; it was our life, my Mom's life. "*How? Not my Mom! Why? No, this can't be true!*", I thought.

He went on to explain that on her CT scan they knew the cancer is in her lymph nodes and where the tumor is located, which is nearly blocking her left airway. He said that once pathology confirms the cancer then the oncologist doctor will come to see her. She will need a PET Scan and that is done as an outpatient. The PET Scan is when they inject isotopes into the body and a full body scan is performed. The isotopes will attach to the cancer throughout the body and light up during the scan.

This will show where the cancer has spread in the body, bones and organs and then decision of a treatment plan can be decided.

I was weeping by this time, completely and utterly heartbroken for my Mom. Brittney was crying too. We hugged each other tightly. The doctor said he was so sorry and they would do everything they could to help her. He also said we could go see her in a few minutes and the nurse would come get us. Through my tears, I asked if we could stay in this room to regain our composure? He said of course and to take all the time we needed.

I was thankful for this small, little white room and the privacy it gave, sheltering us from the other people in the waiting room, across the hallway where we had just been in. I couldn't believe this was happening to my Mom? I couldn't understand why? I desperately wanted to run to her but I also didn't know how I could keep from crying when I did see her. I thought she had escaped the big "*C*" and it was just fluid in her lungs. Of all the people in the world, why my Mom? Not that anyone deserves cancer, no one does. She is such a nice person and definitely didn't deserve this! I thought I had many more years to share with her.

After a few minutes, there was a gentle knock on the door. It was the nurse

"You can go inside her room now."

"We'll be right in".

I wiped my tears and so did Britt. I asked her to please be strong for Grandma when we go see her, she nodded yes, and then we walked into her recovery room. Having gone through an Endoscopy myself, I knew she would be out of it for the rest of the day from the anesthesia and she wouldn't even remember us being there, thankfully.

I walked to her bedside and she smiled at me. She was saying some pretty goofy things and this was the anesthesia talking. As I stood there by her side trying to fight back my tears, it was one of my single most difficult experiences I had to go through, or so I thought. The nurse told us she would be here for a while to recover and then they would bring her back to her room upstairs. I held her hand.

I couldn't breathe. I couldn't think straight. My Mom was so funny and she kept saying silly things to us, making it difficult not to cry and laugh at the same time. She had no idea what Britt and I just found out. Standing in this room, suddenly I was *very* aware there seemed to be a feeling that we were not alone with my Mom, and all I could say it felt like angels stood with us. I got a since of my Nana and Papa were there with all of us. These were her parents. I know this sounds strange, but I know what I felt. I had to lie and tell my Mama that I was going back to work for a meeting and would be back after work. She smiled and said, "Okay sweetie. I will see you later". I told her I loved her, gave her a hug and kiss and then excused myself, as did my daughter. We both left the room weeping. It felt like the world was spinning out of control and I had nothing to grasp onto.

I was a few steps in front of Britt and I clearly remember walking out of that room and into the long, white hallway, I whispered, "I know you are here with my Mom, but I'm not ready to have her leave. Please don't take her now". Britt had caught up to me and I told her that on the main floor of the hospital there is a small meditation chapel and I was going there to get my bearings, as I was in no condition to drive, and asked if she wanted to go with me? She nodded yes. We cried so hard all the way to the chapel. I had my arm around Brittney, to try to comfort her, and to hold onto her for my stability just to walk.

I remember walking past those people that we sat with in the waiting room, as we were obviously weeping. I prayed for their loved ones would be okay and cried harder knowing my

Mama has cancer and wouldn't be okay! We reached the chapel after walking through the hospital maze of hallways and elevators.

We sat together in our silent tears for a while, in this little hospital chapel. I have no idea how long we stayed in the dimly lit chapel of solace. Then I realized, I had to call our family, everyone was waiting to hear the results. I told my daughter I had to leave and to take all the time she needed before she drove. I was going to go home and call our family and then come back when Grandma was awake later. I do not remember walking out of the hospital, getting in my car or driving to my home, but I did. As I drove to my house I realized, I would be the person, to have to call my brother, my sisters, my Auntie M, my Uncle J and my children and to tell them this awful news. It was a feeling of pure dread.

I parked the car, walked into my home and sat down praying for strength to make these phone calls. I knew I had to begin the phone calls. I had to call each family member and share what I was told by the pulmonologist and that he said its cancer. Of course pathology was running the tests to confirm what he visually had seen. I had to repeatedly explain that she has a mass still in her left lung after the Thorentisus, only no one told me. This was just the first part of the diagnosis. Now we know its cancer. We know it's in her lymph nodes. We know what caused the pleural effusion, it's the cancerous mass in her left lung.

As a caring Mom, I had to tell my son Michael about his Grandma and that the doctors would do everything they can to help her. He and Grandma were always so close. They shared such a wonderful relationship together. It broke my heart to have to tell him. Then I had to talk to my daughter Addie, who was also very close. Grandma was Addie's sounding advice board as she grew into a teenager and then later became a mom to Brendon. I called my sisters and by brother to tell them the heartbreaking news and then I had to call my Auntie M and Uncle J to tell them that their big sissy has cancer.

I was in shock. Not understanding this result? I also had to tell everyone that once she is released from the hospital then the PET Scan would be scheduled to see how far the cancer had spread. Once the doctors knew the results, then we all would know what Mom's treatment options would be and go from there.

I had no idea if the group of doctors caring for my Mom already knew it was a severe case of cancer or if they were just really caring and concerned doctors? Everything seemed to happen at a fast pace. Mom had to stay in the hospital until pathology confirmed cancer, and then the oncologist would be up to go over the next phase of things. Two afternoons later, her pulmonologist doctor came in to check on my Mom's breathing, which had gotten better since removing the liquid from her lungs. She was using oxygen to help her breathe, especially if she stood up, her oxygen level would go low into the 80's. Her doctor was very kind as he explained what he had done and that the next part of her medical journey would now be up to the oncologist. The oncologist would be coming soon to explain what was next.

One of my best friends from my teenage days, Michele, was up visiting with my Mom too. Mom was a surrogate mom to my friends growing up. We were having a nice conversation together and with Mom, when the oncologist doctor walked into her room. Our conversations went to silence as we all were waiting for the dreaded results. He introduced himself to my Mom, shook her hand, and shook my hand.

He was a tall middle aged Japanese doctor. He was very nice, but seemed very clinical and matter-of-fact. He stood by my Mom's bed and was going over the results of the Endoscopy procedure and explained where the mass is located, in a main branch of airways, making this an inoperable location. He said given her health history, age, smoking for so many years, that she would not be a candidate for lung removal because her survival rate was not high. He continued to say that all he has been waiting for was pathology to read her biopsy to begin the next phase for treatments.

He told us that he just walked into pathology, brought the doctor the slide and made him read it right then and there, because pathology had not read it yet, and he was frustrated not getting the confirmation of the already *known* results. Hearing this doctor do such a bold thing, made my Mom giggle and so did we. The thought of this very clinical doctor doing this was funny and an appreciated gesture. I was happy he did that for her. The doctor went on to tell Mom that he is sending her home, now that its' confirmed cancer. He is ordering the PET Scan right away, but it may take one week to get approved with Medicare and scheduling the scan.

He said there was no reason my Mom couldn't go home and rest in the comfort of her own home now. He talked to me privately and told me about home care services that he will put a referral in to help us with home care now. We thanked him, as strange as that was to thank the doctor who confirmed to us my Mom has lung cancer.

I told Mom that I was going to walk to Michele's car and see her off and that I would be right back up. Michele, my sweet friend gave her a big hug and said very nice words of encouragement. As I walked down to the parking garage, I was crying so hard. Michele was very supportive to me as well. We said our goodbyes, hugged and I walked back up to the hospital and rode the elevator to the third floor, and walked down the corridor to Mom's room.

Her day nurse was unhooking all of the tubes and IV from my Mom. I helped her get into her clean pajamas and robe. I put her slippers on her feet, put the little white hat on her head and then gathered up the rest of Mom's personal items. The nurse went over the discharge instructions and what tests would come next. I asked the nurse if she was going to be sent home with oxygen. She explained the oxygen numbers that my Mom has would need to have Medicare approve oxygen, and she wasn't a candidate yet based on her oxygen percentages. That didn't make any since to me and I figured I would contact Medicare myself to get her oxygen.

Her nurse asked me to go drive my car to the hospital entrance and she would bring Mom down. I walked down to the parking garage to get my vehicle and drove up to the main entrance of the hospital, where the nurse was waiting with my Mom in a wheelchair. We loaded her in, goy her seatbelt on and I put her bags in the back of the car and away we went. This was Wednesday March 22nd. It was about 6:30p.m., the sun was beginning to set making the sky such a beautiful array of golden colors.

I held my Mom's hand as we drove home and she said,

"Well damn! I knew I didn't feel good, but I wasn't expecting to have cancer!" I agreed with her and told her,

"Mama, we will do whatever you need or want to do. I will call first thing tomorrow and see if I can get you approved through Medicare for the test and then get your test scheduled ASAP."

We held hands all the way home.

We arrived home and I helped her into the house and asked if she wanted to shower tonight and she said, no, she would tomorrow. So I got her settled on the couch and brought her a cup of good coffee. This made her happy. She was very happy to be home. We talked about anything and everything that evening. I asked her if she wanted to get a haircut soon and I could color her hair to make her feel beautiful. She said, "Oh yes please. That would be nice." I knew her vanity level and she was stressed about her grey hair. I wanted her to feel as good as she could.

The next morning I called the phone number for her Medicare plan and explained what had just happened and she needed the approval for the PET Scan. The woman I spoke with was very kind to me. She put me on hold for a few minutes and was able to get authorization immediately. She shared with me she is going through a similar experience with her own mom and this was the least she could do to help. I thanked her from the bottom of my heart and wished her blessings for her and her mom. I then called the Oncology Cancer Center and explained my Mom's story and that I just got approval for the PET Scan and I was hoping for the first available appointment, so she could finally know what she is facing and start healing treatments.

The receptionist was also a very caring woman and she asked,

"Can you get her here at 8:30a.m. tomorrow morning?" I said,

"Yes, of course and thank you."

She gave us directions to the site that actually conducts these special tests and gave us our check in time. I was so overjoyed to get this portion done sooner than later for my Mom's sake. I knew as much as I am worried for her, she was completely worried too.

I called Mom to give her the good news of her appointment for this Friday morning. She was relieved that it was so quick. I assured her that she has the best medical team in San Diego. I told her I loved her and would be home for lunch to check on her. I went to my supervisor and asked to take a very early lunch tomorrow and explained why. He said of course and to take care of my Mom. I was very grateful that my employer was so caring in such a hard personal time of my life. With aging, illness follows some of us. Some families have illness so prevalent that it is so common place and other families are very fortunate to not have to go through repeated illnesses. It meant the world to work for such a caring company and to not have to worry about my job, as I needed to care for my Mom.

Friday morning I got up and made coffee for everyone and got my Mom up and gave her medicines to her. She wasn't up for a shower this morning, so she just got dressed in comfortable clothes. I hugged and kissed my husband and son goodbye and helped my Mom to the car and away we went up to the hospital grounds for her PET Scan.

When we arrived to the hospital campus I asked her if she wanted a wheelchair or did she want the walker with the seat and wheels we got her? The proud woman she was said,

"I'll use the walker." Feeling this was difficult for her, I tried using humor to lighten the moment and pointed out and said,

"Hey Mama, if you get tired, you will have a seat anywhere you want *and* there is a basket to fill with shoes from shopping at the mall."

She laughed at me, because we both knew my mom and her shoe addiction!

When I was about eighteen, Mom and I had gone shopping at the Mission Valley Mall. We were looking for specific clothing for an upcoming event, but not shoes. Mom specifically told me, "Ronda, we are here to find the outfit only. Please keep me away from shoes I don't need anymore." So as we were strolling down the walkway of stores, I was talking to her, or I thought I was, until I realized I was talking to myself! Mom had seen a shoe store SALE and had made an abrupt b-line to that store! We laughed so hard! Like a hummingbird to a flower, smelling the nectar from a mile away, was like my Mom to a shoe sale.

We checked her in and sat down in the small waiting room. A nurse came in and called "Marybeth?" She smiled and assisted my mom to a wheelchair because the test was in a special medical trailer set up specifically for the PET scans. Her nurse told me it would be about forty-five minutes and she would bring her back when she was done. They had given her an IV and injected isotopes. The doctor explained to her that if there is cancer in other parts of her body, these isotopes would gather around the cancer and light up during the full body scan. The scan takes about forty-five minutes to complete.

Once my Mom was in her test, I sat nervously waiting. I was scared that the cancer was in her ribs, because that was the reason I had taken her to the Urgent Care just a week ago. I have always been a positive person, so I was fighting hard to stay positive over this inescapable feeling of dread. Almost on the dot, my Mom came out of the PET Scan. We were told it could take a couple days for the results to be read and provided to her Oncologist to create a treatment plan. We went back to the car and drove home. I got her settled and made her some snacks if she got hungry. I gave her a hug and kiss and said I would see her soon and drove into work.

This was a difficult time at work because we were in the middle of changing our accounting software and would be training the following week on the new system. I was trying to stay focused on my tasks at work, but in the back of my mind, I was really worried about Mom's cancer. Somehow I got through the day at work and hurried home.

It was a happy sight to see my Mom sitting under the umbrella on the patio, sipping a cup of coffee. She smiled as I walked into the back gate and asked me,

"Hi Honey. How was your day?" She had such a big, warm smile.

"My day was good Mama".

I lied and said it was fine and smiled back at her, even though my day was stressful. I joined her in a cup of coffee. It was such a beautiful Spring evening. I knew she wanted her hair dyed and cut, so I asked her if she felt up to going for a haircut and I would color her hair. She smiled and said, "Oh yes!" I took her to our local salon. I brought the walker on wheels in case she needed to sit and rest. I pushed her while she sat comfortably. The salon owner Sharon knew my Mom and treated her like a queen. She cut Mom's hair just the way she liked. I ran next door to buy Mom's hair color, while she was getting pampered. I picked up her beautiful chestnut brown hair color, went back to the salon and we drove home. Mom rested for a bit and then asked me to please color her hair. We had a nice conversation with laughter, of course.

I hadn't colored her hair in years. It was during the application of the dye that I felt two huge bumps on her scalp. One of them was like the size of a walnut. I tried to be nonchalant and asked,

"Mom, do you know you have two big bumps on your head?", She replied,

"Oh yes. I have had them for a while."

This alarmed me, but I had my poker face on for her, even though I was freaking out inside. Somehow, we all managed to get through the weekend. My Mom and I watched our favorite ghost shows and Ron and I went shopping for things to help my Mom at home with. We went and purchased a shower chair with handles, if she was weak, she could sit and enjoy a shower still and feel safe. We also got for the shower instant shower bars that suction cup to the tile, so she would extra stability.

On Sunday night we made a wonderful family dinner and a favorite of Mom's. We made stuffed cabbage rolls using her best friend, Marylou's recipe. We dined at the table together, the four of us and shared lovely conversations. It was nice to see my Mom eating, as her appetite had greatly diminished. We laughed because she ate two cabbage rolls! She commented on how good she felt and how much she *loved* her haircut and color. She said it made her feel beautiful again.

I'm sure it was in the back of her head that we would know her final diagnosis of cancer tomorrow, but she never mentioned it. It was in my head too. I was so worried. I loved her so much and this was just not fair. It was getting late in the evening and I made sure she had her medicines before I went to bed. Mom now wanted pain medicine regularly, and I made certain she was comfortable. I hugged and kissed her goodnight and told her I would call the Oncologist's office when they opened to see if I could get any answers. She thanked me.

I cried when I went upstairs. This had been a constant thing I was doing since she went in the hospital, was to cry in the privacy of my bedroom. My whole life I tried to be strong and not let my emotions get the best of me. But this experience with my Mom was far different emotionally for me, than anything I had ever faced. I wanted to get the results I think as much as my Mom needed to hear them, so that her treatment could begin right away.

Monday morning March 26th, this would be the day of finally knowing Mom's cancer diagnosis and stage. I woke up early, got ready for work and went and made her a continental breakfast and brought her breakfast in bed and her medicines. She laughed at me and said,

"Honey you don't need to do this for me." I smiled and replied,

"Mama, you are a queen and allow me to treat you like one."

I gave her a hug and kiss and said I would let her know as soon as I heard anything.

For anyone that is going through this similar situation, waiting for the diagnosis is difficult. All you want to do is have the doctors hurry up with the results so that your loved one can begin healing and getting better. Just the word cancer brings up all sorts of scary thoughts and to be stuck in a sort of limbo, makes it challenging to cope. There is never a good cancer to get. Cancer is bad but the human spirit is good. Staying positive can help. I had to remind myself of staying positive. Usually, being positive, is a characteristic trait of mine and one that I have mastered in my lifetime of challenges and hurdles. In this cancer limbo, I had to make myself stay positive and have hope.

I was a clock watcher that morning. I knew the oncologist's office didn't open until 9:00a.m., so I kept very busy at work getting ready for training that would start the following day. I was trying to keep the feeling of dread from over powering my thoughts. Finally, 9:00a.m. on the dot. I called right when the office opened and talked to the receptionist. I asked her to please have Mom's doctor call me when he had her PET Scan results and I gave her my cell number and office phone number. She assured me he would call, I thanked her and resumed working.

I called Mom on her cell and let her know that I have a message into him and suggested to take a nap while we waited. She said she was tired and that sounded good. I could hear in her voice, she was worried too. Who wouldn't be? So we waited. Knowing what this doctor did with her pathology tests at the hospital I was comforted in knowing, he was very hands on and compassionate would not let his patients wait on test results that are life changing.

Two hours later my cell phone started to vibrate. I looked at it and knew it was the doctor's office by the number. I answered quickly and it was the doctor. I was already walking downstairs from my office to go out back into the yard. I knew I needed to be alone for these words he was about to say to me. I let him know I was trying to get somewhere private, and I quickly made it outside.

All of a sudden, it felt like time stood still. As my heartbeat raced from anxiety, I could hear it beating. *Boom boom! Boom boom!* Then he began telling me about her cancer diagnosis. In a gentle voice he said "Ronda. The results from the PET Scan have been reviewed. I am sorry to say, we knew there was a large tumor in her lung and we knew from the tests at the hospital that the cancer had reached some lymph nodes. We now know that the cancer has spread through her entire body. It's in all of her lymph nodes, it's in her spine, it's in her ribs, it's in her pelvis, and it's in her liver, it's in her kidneys and in her brain."

The shocking news of these words being spoken to me, made my world get very small in a split second. He continued to tell me what I feared the most, he said,

"I'm sure you want to know her time line?" I said,

"Yes I need to know."

"She has stage four terminal cancer. Given her health from the hospital and these results, I would estimate she has about seven to nine months left."

I interrupted him, "What? Did you say she has months left to live?" That's when the tears flowed down, like rain flowing in a river downstream. I didn't care I was outside in the back of my office. I didn't care who was going to see or hear me. My brain couldn't wrap around this information he was telling me. I asked him,

"Is there anything we can do to help her?" He said,

"Her options are but a few. She would not survive removing her lung, so that is not an option. The cancer has spread to her entire body that even if she was strong enough for chemotherapy, she might not survive chemo. An otherwise healthy person before they are diagnosed with cancer, will get very ill from chemo and they will have the fight of their life. Your Mom who already has a weakened heart and combined with her age, chemo may diminish what's left of her life and take away any quality she might have. She will need to decide quality versus quantity."

I asked him what her other options were and he said simply, "To let it run its course". Wow, not what I wanted to hear! He offered to call and tell her and I volunteered to be the person to tell her, she was *my* Mom. I thought it may be gentler coming from me than from the very nice but very clinical oncologist. I told him that she will need to make her own decision of what she wants to do and that I can't make that choice for her. He said he will make an appointment this Friday and we can all meet and she can make her decision. We hung up. I was standing there just stunned.

    I walked back into my office and my friend Angie looked over at me with concern. She knew what that call was because we had a brief chat about everything earlier. I looked at her and shook my head, with tears in my eyes, and shook my head in a gesture of *no*. I walked to my supervisor's office and through the tears I told him my Mom has stage four terminal cancer. I asked him if I could please leave and take a long lunch now, so I could tell her. He, of course said yes.

    I grabbed my purse and car keys and dialed my husband's cell phone. I couldn't face this alone. I didn't know how to tell my sweet Mama she had terminal cancer and that she was given only months left to live. My husband didn't answer his phone. I drove home on autopilot and I remember turning onto my street and calling Ron one more time. Just as I turned left into our driveway of our condos, I happened to look in my rearview mirror. By a miracle, Ron was pulling in right behind me. He had just finished his first shift of work.

    I let him park his car and waited for him to hop in mine. I didn't even need to utter a word, he knew by the look on my face and the tears rolling down my cheeks, it wasn't good news. I parked at our townhouse and said, " I have to tell my Mom she's dying. This sucks!" I got out of the car, opened the back gate and walked into the house. Mom was lying on the couch watching some TV. I tried to be brave and have a poker face on, so she didn't need to witness a blubbering crying daughter. This was about her life, her end of the journey. I just happen to be her daughter and share a lifetime. I tried to be strong.

I walked over to her and knelt down on the floor next to her and said,

"Mama, I talked to your oncologist." She asked me,

"Oh? What did he say?"

You could see she in her eyes she was concerned, but *she* was trying to be the strong mom for me. I began to tell her the hardest words that would ever come out of my mouth. "Mama. your PET Scan showed the cancer has spread through your whole body. It's in your bones, your spine, your ribs, your liver, your kidneys. He said that its stage four terminal cancer. This is why your ribs hurt so much and why you have been extra tired."

It was at this point when I completely lost it. I was crying so hard. I laid my head in her lap crying uncontrollably. I told her how sorry I was. How this wasn't fair. I said "He said you have seven to nine months left Mama and your only options are chemo or natural". I kept apologizing to her. I'm sorry, I'm so sorry. As I had my head lying in her lap, she stroked my face and I just hugged her. Then I asked the stupidest question. I asked her,

"Mama, are you going to haunt me like on the ghost shows we watch?" She laughed and said,

"No honey, I won't haunt you, but you will know I am there." I replied,

"Well flick the lights on and I will know it's you."

She agreed. This made us laugh nervously, but at least there was a tiny glimmer of laughter in an otherwise solemn moment in life.

She surprised me with what she said next. "I've always wondered if it would be better to know if you are going to die or not? I think it's better to know, because then everyone can say their goodbyes, rather than dying abruptly without warning. I have lived a good loving life. I have a wonderful, big family, wonderful kids, grand kids and great grand kids and good friends. It's okay." And yes she was a Mom of five, four surviving, a Grandma of twelve and a Great-Grandma or Oma of seventeen!

I calmed down a bit and she was in shock over the news. I told her that we will go on Friday to the Cancer Center and you can let the oncologist know what you want to do. She said immediately,

"I'm not having chemo! I know that. I watched what it did to my friend Sue and I don't want to go through that. I want to enjoy what time I have left."

"Mama, it's okay if you don't want to go through chemo. This is completely your choice."

I let her know that we will support her and any decision she wants. This is a very difficult choice and it was hers' and hers' alone to make. I would just love her.

CHAPTER 3 - ACCEPTANCE, REFLECTIONS & WILLS

After hearing the shocking news of being diagnosed with terminal stage four cancer, then having to deal with the irrevocable and unwanted term of ,you have months to live, this can become one of the hardest parts of this journey for your loved one who is the terminally ill person and for the family and friends that are affected with the pending loss.

In this day and age of medicines, treatments and surgeries, you think to yourself that there *must* be something that can be done? You will begin to question the death sentence that has been given to your spouse, your parent, your sister, your brother or your child , your friend or yourself. There must be a medicine that can take away the illness? There must be some secret treatment somewhere in the world to save my beloved family member? As you are thinking these things, so is the person that is sick. The reality of one's mortality sets in.

I have experienced death of my Papa when I was in my early twenties, the death of friends dying too young in car accidents and my Nana four years after my Papa. For my friends that died to young it was hard to deal with, so young and suddenly taken, it seemed cruel and unfair. When it was my Papa, he was the rock of our wonderful family and that hit me so hard. There was a tiny bit of solace in knowing he had lived a long good life, and I still wanted him to be here in life. When my Nana passed, it was comforting to know she was with Papa again, her soul mate, and that she didn't have to suffer any more from Alzheimer's that robbed her of everything.

It doesn't matter who the loved one is that's beginning this unknown journey ahead, you don't want them to go and definitely not like this. Knowing you will lose them in a term of "months" is even harder to accept. So many questions begin and there just aren't any good answers, at this point it seems. There can be anger, shock and an emotional vortex begins making you feel like your world is spinning all around, out of control, even though you are standing still.

Having gone through this journey with my Mom is why I share the deepest and very personal experience. I want to help anyone to make the most of what time is left and to make the most of what you can. Time becomes so precious. Spoken words, family histories and funny stories are what will matter the most later. These are the moments that have created the memories of life shared together. They are also what will be missed knowing there will be no more memories to make and share in the future with your loved one.

As much as I wanted to move Heaven and Earth to save my Mom, I could not make her decision of her treatment. I had to support her in the choice she made of no chemotherapy. I couldn't be selfish and make her suffer through chemotherapy because *I* wanted her with me longer. She didn't want *that* sickness and I had to support her choice. I had to accept her choice, no matter what, just as she had accepted this very raw deal of the terminal cancer diagnosis, with courage, grace and laughter. The sooner that there is acceptance, the sooner you and your family can really enjoy the life that is left.

I'm a "fixer. I have always tried to make the best out of even the worst situations. I couldn't fix this one. I couldn't make Mom free of cancer. I cried every night privately in my bedroom since she first was admitted to the hospital and every night since knowing her fate. I never wanted her to know how scared I was or she would worry about me. I didn't know what was going to truly happen to her and neither did she. I had to be strong for her just as she was once the strong and loving Mom for me. She was not perfect, she was not a Saint, but she was *my* mom whom I love.

March 26th was the date that we found out how ill she was, and it's also the date that changed *everything* of how we looked at life and death. Mom has always been a spiritual person, so this helped her along her journey. I was a believer in something more than us, definitely spiritual. This faith was something to draw on, for some comfort.

This day was also my grandson Josh's birthday. He turned five on this day. We had committed to going to Britt's house for just a family celebration and no one wanted to disappoint Josh. Oma loved her great grandbabies, all of them and was not going to let him be disappointed. So, away we piled into the FJ and went to wish Josh a happy birthday. When we arrived, Josh squealed in delight that Oma was at his house! It was very sweet. I walked into the kitchen and Britt followed me. I gave her a big hug and whispered to her,

"I am so sorry baby. Grandma didn't want to make Josh sad or we would not have come. She is going to let me know when she needs to go. Okay?"

"Yes, okay momma".

Britt nodded her head, yes. We both had to fight the tears away.

I took sweet pictures of the Britt, Addie and Michael with Grandma and with Jake, Josh and Brendon. We helped sing "Happy Birthday Joshua" and he opened his presents with such happiness. We may have been there twenty minutes and I could see that Mom was tired. I sat down next to her and asked if she would like to go? She said, "Yes please." Everyone hugged and kissed goodbye.

This same evening, after we all had time to digest the news. After the endless phone calls to my brother, sisters, to Auntie M and then to Uncle J, her sister and brother, and finally to Marylou, my Mom's best friend, The M & M's. Once I could just be with my Mom, we began the most important conversations with each other. Being the person I am and the person my Mom was, we had to spin this from a death sentence into what are the most meaningful things to experience in life. What are the special places to explore, visits with friends, anything and everything began to emerge of my Mom's wishes.

As sad as I was knowing these would be *the last* of everything for her and for me, as her daughter. I got a notepad out to write down what her wishes were. They were simple and sweet. She wanted to see her kids and grandkids. She wanted to see her brother and her sister. She wanted to go to Catalina. To go to Barona Casino with Marylou and not Las Vegas (my Mom LOVED gambling). She wanted to go to the Botanical Gardens at Balboa Park and see the fish pond and go to Ocean Beach. So I began her wish list and would do everything in my power to make it happen.

She talked about Christmas and she wanted to give all her grand-children and the great grandchildren a book of photos of her, so they would always know who she was and remember her. I told her I would make that happen, as I am also a photographer. I figured I would take a series of pictures of her, when she felt up to photos. She started sharing with me stories of her youth and of her life. It was fun to hear about her beautiful petticoats she would wear under her skirts when she was a teenager in the 1950's going to Hoover High School. Or hearing about her first car and her trips to the beach with her friends. To hear about her dad freaking out about her navy blue and white striped bathing suit with no back and he made her put a shirt on!

This began a whole new idea and one I highly recommend doing with your loved one. We named it, The Forget Me Not Book. I went and bought index cards and an index box. Then I started writing questions on the top of each card, of things about my Mom. For instance her ten favorite smells, her ten favorite foods, her first kiss, her first boyfriend, her favorite memory of my brother Michael, of my sister Crystal, of my sister Diana and of me. I would then turn these cards into a book to share, so Marybeth, Mom, Grandma, Oma would always be remembered.

The titles went on and on. What this created was a fun and funny experience that I could share with my Mom or that my kids could share with their Grandma. In the evenings while she lay on the living room sofa, all comfortable, I would pull out the index cards and randomly pick a few cards. I would ask Mom the questions and she would tell me stories of her life. I would write them down as she spoke.

I thought I had heard all of her growing up stories, until doing this with her. It was a good way for her to enjoy herself, fill her heart with loving, happy memories too. This would keep her mind focused on memories and not on her illness, and gave her reflections of the wonderful life she has had lived and the people she loved and shared life with. Videos of these moments would be an ideal time to do this. To create a family record of who they were, where they came from and to have these memories to re-visit in the future, these become priceless. Time is something you can't have back or hearing their voice, or their laughter.

When Mom spoke and she shared her special events of her life and the silly stories of when she was young. She had such a sparkle in her eyes and joy in her voice. This was so good to see and feel. I looked forward to hearing her stories and you could see she felt good sharing them. It was such a wonderful bonding time, sharing her lifetime memories.

In the back of my head, I knew one reason I also needed this information. So I could have more to remember my Mom by and to give these memories to my family that live out of state. I felt blessed to have shared life over the last decade with Mom, living with my family. I always enjoyed her and she was a bright light to be around.

Mom, my husband Ron and Marylou made a date to go to the Barona Casino together in a couple weeks. Have a nice lunch and play some slot machines. The two M & M's *loved* gambling and Mom was always very lucky and would win a lot. Being her daughter I shared in the luck as well. But mostly, I knew this was something that was meaningful to her, and that brought her joy. It was good to have something to look forward to as well.

During this week after her final diagnosis, her oncologist had already signed her up for in home care. The nurse assigned to Mom came out on Tuesday, March 27th. I took my lunch time early from work so I could be at the first meeting and ask any question we had. The woman was very kind and compassionate. She told us the way that the services could help my Mom.

Mom was going to get a health aide to come help with showers, as my Mom just didn't feel strong enough to do this simple task anymore, most of us take for granted. Even though I was willing to help care for my Mom, she was a prideful woman. It was a relief to her to have the home aide and provided a since of her own modesty. I understood that and respected that privacy. She would also get all of the medical care she needed. Her nurse would report to her oncologist as treatment goes along. I explained that between my husband and I, we were going to work around our work schedules and the home care people so that my Mom was not going to have to be alone. It was a welcomed relief to find out of the extent of the services available to help her.

During this week, we were able to sit and have family dinners together. I asked Mom what she would like to eat and she named some soups, like potato soup and vegetable barley. So I prepared two big pots of soup and put them in easy to serve containers. I froze most of them. They were easy access for her or the home aide to prepare a nutritious meal. We also bought her chocolate drinks that added the extra vitamins and minerals, designed for seniors. These actually tasted bad. So I went looking at Costco and found their chocolate weight loss shakes and they contained the right amount of vitamins and minerals. Mom didn't need to lose weight, but needed the extra nutrition. She actually enjoyed the taste over the ones geared for older adults.

In this week, we accomplished some big things for Mom and her care at home. The nurse had set up more appointments this week and I told her Friday would be her follow up with her oncologist and we would go from there. Her nurse said to please let her know as soon as possible, so she can make sure that Mom gets all the needed care.

Mom was so courageous. Her spirit was strong and we laughed and shared so much this week. She told me one evening,

"You know, as much as I don't want cancer, it is what it is. We will make the most of all of this time".

"Mama, we will definitely make the best of the time, I promise!"

I assured her we would. I didn't see her cry this week, but I'm sure privately she did. Probably not to let me see she was scared. I know I cried privately every night, for the same reason. I was scared for her and for losing her.

If I felt I wasn't ready to let her go, I couldn't begin to understand how she felt? I'm sure there are more stages of disbelief, grief of letting go, anger, sadness but not of pity, but sadness of your family you have to say goodbye to them. For some divine reason both Mom and I took everything day to day, with smiles, stories, love and laughter and cups of coffee. We began making the most of life as best as we could and depending on how she felt. Every awake minute counted.

It's hard to look back after an a loss that has happened, and it's very easy to say, "I would have. I could have. I should have." No one healthy or ill, should have to feel regret of something they *should have* or *would have* done in life. I felt my own would've, should've and could've after I found out my Mom was so ill. I wanted to turn back the clock one year and start over. But that was not an option. I made a choice at this point to live for the moment. Live for the hug. Live for silly laughter after sharing a funny story. Live in the moment just like my Mom was doing. Time was so precious and priceless. We both knew that.

We even discussed about when she passes. Oh, this was not a comfortable topic, but a necessary one. Her case nurse highly suggested we do a Living Will. A Living Will is basically the patients Advance Care Directive of what they want medically done for them. This document preserves their wishes. We did complete this with my Mom's wishes and that was to not resuscitate if she had a heart attack or something like that. My Mom wanted to go peacefully and not live on life support.

Having to place the Living Will on my refrigerator with the emergency number's to reach her doctors was a hard thing to do. I held in my hands my Mom's life wishes. Her choice to not be revived, her choice to go, and it was not easy to not beg her, "Please allow them to care for you. I don't want you to die!" That was the irrational, emotional side of me thinking those thoughts, because I knew what she meant and why. She didn't want to be an invalid. She wanted to be in control of her body, her mind and not a machine breathing every breath for her. I feel the same way.

Her nurse also asked if my Mom had a Last Will & Testament. Strange that it just was never a topic in my family. Mom no longer had her Businesses or properties as she once had earlier in life. My idea of a will, was it was meant for people to leave their large amounts of money or properties to their family or people of their choosing. I also found out that a Power of Attorney lasts only until the moment of someone dying and a Will names an Executor that can fulfill the last wishes and handle all items regarding the person who passed and handle their estate. In the Will it can outline burial or cremation choices, which is important to have.

To really *know* what your loved one wants, while they can think, talk and make decisions, this can help later when emotions are so raw. There are great websites that you can get free forms to help create these documents. Type in free will forms on the internet and you will find many choices and information to help. Make sure you look for your particular state's laws and you can consult your lawyer. To have these matter resolved in a time of clarity and without the extreme emotions after someone passes, can really help.

One last part of this matter is pre-planning the services. For instance if you know what your loved wants, let's say cremation. If you look in your area, do a Better Business check, to make sure they are a good caring business that doesn't take advantage of families at their lowest and most vulnerable time. Grief is a tough road to walk. Having your own arrangements completed, even if you are not sick, should be done to help your surviving family.

I was very lucky to have the company we chose, only I didn't know I could have pre-planned and that simply means to by preplanning, you know what your loved one wanted and your own emotions won't be overcome with buying anything like a golden crypt, because they deserve the best. It is a big relief and a recommended doing this before the latter. You can think clearer, sort of. All of these processes are difficult and will never be easy, however, by taking care some of these things now, they can help you later when you are actually facing the loss.

That evening Mom and I had the conversations about what she would want, I said

"Mama. This is not a fun subject, but I want to honor your wishes of what you want after you go."

"Honey, I want to be cremated. I don't want some over the top funeral. I want a Celebration of Life."

"Okay Mama, anything you want. I love you."

This helped knowing and when we were preparing her Last Will and Testament, which was so difficult to do, it was her simple wishes. She didn't want any problems after she was gone and I prepared what she wanted and how she wanted it. Once I had it typed, we needed to get it notarized and witnessed. I was in process of doing that, as we had time.

It was a big relief for my Mom and for me to have this part of the journey completed. Now we could visit and do anything my Mom wanted to do. We didn't need to talk about the cancer, unless she wanted to talk about it. She looked so much better than when she had gone into the hospital originally, but she didn't have a lot of extra energy. She slept a lot and she ate lightly. She was still drinking her coffee, which brought us both humor and this was good. We knew if she drank her coffee, then she was alright.

Her nurse came out on Thursday afternoon while I was at work and she called me about her visit with my Mom. She was a bit surprised that in two days how my Mom seemed a bit more tired and I agreed with her. But who wouldn't feel tired and depressed when they had just been told they had 7-9 months left? Her nurse said she was going to call in the report to her oncologist. I reminded her that we see him tomorrow and I will let her know what he says.

When I came home from work, Mom was sitting in the patio and drinking her coffee. She also was smoking, which at this point, it was not going to give her more cancer and our whole family agreed if it brings her stress relief then let her be. She is allowed to do anything she wants. It was on this lovely afternoon that my Mom made a strange statement. She said,

"I just love the Springtime out of all the seasons. The flowers blooming, the birds singing, the skies are beautiful. I love where we live and this is a happy home. I love to come out and sit in the sunshine and look across the street to our short Rocky Mountains."

"It is beautiful Mom".

The view from her patio chair was of the purple jacaranda trees in the condos and the beautiful rocky hillside across the street from our home. The blue skies always seemed so striking against the little rocky mountains.

She continued talking, "Sweetie if I have to go now, I'm glad it's in the Spring, it's my favorite season". Immediately red flags were running through my head, waving with great imaginary force. I thought, *What does she mean if she has to go, she's glad it's in the Spring? She has seven to nine months?* And then I told myself to disregard it, she was just sharing feelings.

We had a nice family dinner of homemade potato soup, knowing Mom loved this soup and she would eat it. We had a nice visit and shared some laughs. We truly enjoyed each other. We had dinner on the patio on this lovely Spring evening. The birds chirping and the two hummingbirds came for a visit too. The spiritual humming birds. They have a great meaning to our family. After my Nana passed and joined her beloved Papa, my Mom, my Auntie M and I all began having two distinct hummingbirds visit us. It's been a wonderful experience.

We all had lived in different parts of the country when this began occurring. There is a difference of seeing a hummingbird fly near you for the nectar of a flower and when they visit *you* and fly a foot in front of your face looking into your eyes, hovering for a minute. Once my Mom, my Auntie M and I all discovered we all had these sweet and repeated feathered visitors, we all agreed it was Nana and Papa's spirits coming to say hi. This brought us all comfort.

I could see Mom was getting tired and tomorrow would be a big emotional day for her at the Cancer Center. I suggested I could tuck her in and give her the evening medicines. She told me that sounded like a great idea. She was tired. So I turned the bed down and picked out some soft and comfy pajamas for her. I helped her change, as she seemed weaker. And I disregarded it and thought she will be all right, she's just tired.

The next morning I went to bring her some juice, coffee and a bagel in case she was hungry and served it on a bed tray, before I left for work. I reminded her that a health aide would be her at 10:00am for a shower. My Mom smiled and said oh that will be good. I gave her a hug and kiss as I was walking out of her bedroom and said I would see her at 2:00pm to take her up to the Cancer Center. I blew her a kiss and she smiled and blew one back.

When I was at work, later that day, we had a company meeting that the President was conducting and discussing our new policies. During the meeting he discussed PTO (paid time off)and that with the new changes you can donate some of your time to another co-worker, as you couldn't carry over a certain amount of hours into the next year. He went on to say, "Ronda is going through a very tough time if you haven't heard. If any of you would like to donate time to her you can." He looked at me and asked, "Is that okay?" In near tears, I said yes and thank you.

After the meeting my dear friend Angie and a fellow co-worker offered to help pick up Marylou from Pacific Beach and bring her to visit on any weekend my Mom was up to it. She said, "I know with your Fibromyalgia it's hard for you in the evenings and I would like to help." I hugged and thanked her. She offered for this weekend that she was available Saturday and she would call Marylou to make arrangements. I said, "That would be amazing. I will make them lunch and they can visit until Mom gets tired. She will be so happy to see her!" I told her I would talk to her later as I had to leave for Mom's appointment.

As I drove away from my office, I couldn't shake the feeling I was having. It was a feeling of heaviness maybe because my Mom's cancer, but I somehow knew it wasn't just that. I watched Mom every day this week sleep more each day, where it seemed she began sleeping more than she was awake. I had to remind myself to ask her oncologist about it and about getting oxygen for her.

I arrived home and went inside to pick Mom up. She seemed weak and shaky to walk, so I got her the walker on wheels for her. It had a nice padded seat, so if she was dizzy or weak, it would allow her to sit anytime. I helped her outside and got her loaded into my FJ and placed the walker in the back and away we went up towards the hospital. We arrived at the Cancer Center, this was located on the hospital grounds. Thankfully there was a special patient loading area that was flat and only 10 feet to go inside the Cancer Center.

I told Mom that I was going to get a wheelchair, so she could be more comfortable. Mom had no problem with this. I walked inside the doors into the beautiful, soothing lobby. I got a wheelchair and went back outside to get Mom seated. I told her I will bring her inside then go park and I would be right back. I wheeled her inside and pushed the wheelchair next to a seat.

As I drove into the parking structure again this month, I laughed and said out loud "Sadly, I do need my own parking spot at this hospital". I parked and walked as quick as my body would let me and met up with my Mom. I signed in for her appointment. The staff in this office, were amazing and very compassionate. That brought great comfort to us.

Within five minutes a nurse came out and called out,

"Marybeth?"

"That's me." Mom said,

The nurse came out and wheeled her into a patient room, as I followed. She asked Mom some questions and told us the doctor would be here in just a moment, and he was. He was as punctual as he was clinical. We were glad this is the same doctor from the hospital. He makes things happen and he understands what time wasted could mean to a family.

He listened to her lungs a few times and said the fluid is back on her lungs, so before we left, he wanted to schedule a

Thorentisus and help relief the pressure she's feeling with every breath. He was surprised to see her in the wheelchair and I explained that she had a few good days after the hospital, but each day this week she has been more tired and is sleeping more than she's awake. He asked about her appetite and I said she is trying to eat and I have prepared all natural homemade soups for her. He said that's good.

He then began to ask the question of treatment choices,

"Have you decided Marybeth what you want to do?" She replied,

"Yes. I have decided that I don't want chemo. I feel it would make me sicker and I just want to go natural."

Even though I knew her choice, hearing her say it knocked the wind from my sail and tugged on my heart. He gave a brief synopsis of chemo statistics vs. natural. He also said that he would do anything that she wanted to try. He went on to say, "When a patient is given a couple years to live, they could pass in a week. When another patient is given a week to live, they can live two more years". Each person is different.

He had scheduled the Thorentisus and an x-ray, then took my Mom back. She was as surprised as I was to have this procedure again and so soon. About thirty minutes later, she was wheeled back in the room by her doctor. He said as nicely as he could relay to my Mom, "Given that you are only one week out of the hospital, and that you needed another Thorentisus so soon, along with your other symptoms of sleeping more, which is all part of it. I'm sorry but I have prepare you and need to change the time line down to 4-6 months."

He went on to tell us that he is going to call Hospice in at this point. In my head I heard the word *Hospice* and was freaking out inside. Hospice = Death. I looked at my Mom and held her hand. She said,

"Well, this is not what I wanted to hear. Dammit cancer!"

"I am so sorry Mom."

What else can you say at a moment like this? Her doctor said Hospice may call tonight or this weekend. I shook his hand and said thank you and we left. This was just supposed to be an appointment to discuss her options, but not another Thorentisus or a discussion of a shortened amount of life!

    We drove home she said to me, "Well at least we know. I'm shocked that I have less time." I told her how sorry I was and we would make the best of the time we have together. The rest of the car ride home was silent. I figured my Mom needed some quiet time for her own reflection of this shocking news from the oncologist. I didn't turn the radio on for fear of what songs would play making these feelings worse. I had to find my own strength and courage right now for her and not burst into tears. I figured I could fall apart some other time, because right now my Mom needed me, and I would do anything for her.

    I drove down the highway 125 that comes down the hill to overlook Santee. All of the beautiful short rocky mountains, as my Mom and I would call them. I knew this was a beautiful site for her to see. The place we have loved and called home for many years now. We arrived home and I told her I would call the family so she didn't have to worry about that. This was already hard enough for her to wrap her head around that fact she has terminal cancer, but to find out now her time has been shortened. I didn't want my Mom to have to suffer any more heartache.

    My son Michael was home and Ron was getting ready to leave for a short shift at work. I had to tell them what the doctor said and hugged my son so tight. He told me he was sorry and we cried. I hugged my husband and said, "I just can't believe this is happening." They both hugged Grandma, as we fondly called her. I called my daughters and asked if they wanted to come over so I could talk to them about Grandma. Each of them both said, "No, please tell me now." I told them what happened and repeated what the oncologist said.

My daughters cried and I tried to comfort each of them. They both said they would come by tomorrow to visit Grandma. I understood, they both had small kids and busy schedules to work around. I told them I loved them and that I would send their to love to Grandma.

Michael was leaving to go out with his dad and offered to stay home. I said,

"No honey. It will be good if you go out. We will be fine. I love you."

"Mom, I love you too," he said.

My husband also offered to stay home and I told him, "It will be okay and I need this time with her. I love you." He said he loved me and held me tight. He gave Mom a big hug too.

I got her settled on the sofa and went in the kitchen to make coffee. A small amount of solace for her, she loved her coffee. I asked her if she was hungry and she said no. I understood. Sometimes food can fill a void during a time of stress and other times food is the last on the list. As the coffee was brewing I sat on the other side of our L shaped sofa and asked her,

"Would margaritas sound better than coffee right now?" She laughed and said,

"Maybe later."

The two of us sat together sharing a cup of coffee and we also shared an incredible conversation about life. There was nothing in the world that meant more to me than to be right there with my Mom, in our house, talking and laughing about nothing and yet about everything. In times of trouble or sadness our family has always tried to find the bright side to situations.

When other people cry for sadness, we do cry but somehow find silly stories and humor to comfort each other with laughter. Maybe it's just our family's way of coping?

    I asked Mom if she wanted to watch our ghost shows tonight. She said, "Oh yes, lets watch them." So we hunkered down on the sofa and watched our favorite show together. After the first show ended, she said, "Sweetie, I am tired and I'm going to bed." I understood and got her the evening medicines and said I would record the other shows for her.

    I brought in her pillows and comforter from the living room and got her settled in her bed. I hugged and kissed her good night. I put her cell phone on her night stand and said to call me if she needed anything during the night. I locked up the house, recorded the ghost shows, went upstairs to my bedroom and collapsed on my bed from emotional exhaustion.

    I lay there for about five minutes to collect myself, knowing I had to make the round of phone calls to my Auntie M and my Uncle J. Then I had to call my sisters and brother and Marylou, to share the updated news of my Mom. I finally felt I could make the phone calls and proceeded with calling Auntie M first. I told her how the doctor appointment went and that she had more fluid built up on her lungs, so she had another Thorentisus performed. After her examination and given her steady decline from just last week, he reduced her time line to 4 to 6 months! I started crying and so did my Auntie. I told her I was sorry and it's just not fair.

    She said to me that she was going to see about coming down from Portland next week for a visit. She had been planning to come to visit after her trip to St. Thomas, where her other home is, but she wants to come now. She asked me to find a manicurist that will come to the house so her big sissy can get pampered, and I said I have a friend Melody that is a cosmetologist that I would ask. Auntie went on to tell me she would call Uncle J for me and share the news. I thanked her because I still had four more calls to make and it's just so hard.

Having to call my sisters and my brother to tell them our Mom only had such a short time to live was so difficult. My brother had moved up to Spokane last year to be closer to his daughters and grandchildren and both of my sisters lived in Burlington, Iowa. I repeated the new information and they all said they were all going to do their best to come see Mom. The news was shocking to hear from the doctor and it felt surreal to tell my family.

I called Marylou next. She said she had been worried all day. I apologized for not calling sooner, but it was just too emotionally hard to talk. I repeated the doctor's appointment new information and had to gently tell her that her best friend would only be with us a very short time more. She told me that she thought something was wrong because my Mom hadn't answered her cell phone.

These two remarkable women, the two M & M's shared such a wonderful friendship. They met while Mom was an office manager in Old Town for a jewelry business and Marylou owned her own Aerospace employment service. They met only six years before, but shared so much together in that time. They would talk every night on the phone for about an hour. Mom would often go spend the weekend down at Marylou's house in Pacific Beach. They took numerous Las Vegas trips together and just really enjoyed each other's company.

I told Marylou that Angie offered to pick her up to come out and see Mom for a visit this weekend, if she was up to it. She said yes and Saturday would be good, she would like that very much. We hung up and I just cried. Sitting in my bedroom just weeping for my Mom. It was five days ago we found out my Mom was terminal and today we find out she is sicker than originally thought. I couldn't stop crying. How could this happen to my sweet Mom? No one deserves cancer and from all the people in the world not her. *How could I go on without her*, I thought.

      She was always such a happy woman even when life held its enormous challenges and hurdles to jump over. She never complained about anything or about anyone. I called Angie to update her and asked if we could arrange tomorrow for Marylou to come visit and she said yes, of course. I thanked her and then hung up. No more talking, no more calls. I lay on my bed that evening waiting for my husband to get home from work and cried for hours. I was always a strong woman, like my Mom. I tried to control my emotions throughout my life, but tonight I just let them go wherever they needed to go. I had to release the heartache and pending loss I was feeling.

      I remember thinking that any birthday or holiday this year would be the last to have with my Mom. I broke down to my lowest point and feeling desperate, I prayed. It had been a very long time since I prayed. At one time I was very religious and then it became more of a spiritual belief. After my Papa passed, something had changed in me. I prayed for my Mom to not suffer. I prayed for strength to help her through whatever she faced. I soon fell asleep

CHAPTER 4 - HOSPICE

Saturday, March 31st, Hospice day. I woke up from complete sleep, to sitting straight up with a jolt. Like a force of life buzzed my body. I had to get my bearings of what day it was and that it was not a bad dream I had about my Mom having terminal cancer, it was real. Thinking it was a work day. I soon realized it was Saturday morning. "Thank God!" I thought. My eyes were swollen from crying the night before. I went downstairs and started coffee for everyone. I prepared a food tray with some toast, water and a chocolate nutrition drink with a straw in it. I placed my Mom's morning medicines, including her pain pills and walked to her room. I knocked gently and opened the door. She was awake.

She was sitting up on her bed. I smiled as I walked towards her bed, I said,

"Good Morning Mama! How are you doing? Do you need your pain medicine?" I asked.

She said, "I'm okay. I slept good and yes I would like the medicine."

I handed her the medicine and sat on the edge of the bed. She smiled and replied,

"Oh sweetie that's so nice of you. You didn't need to do all this".

"Yes I do need to treat you like this. You are the Queen so start taking advantage of this!"

We had a nice little giggle with each other. She took a few sips of the chocolate drink and then took her medicines. She said she wasn't hungry yet. I told her not to worry.

"It's just so hard to get me head wrapped around this."

I replied, "I know Mama. I know how I am feeling and just can't image how you are? I'm so sorry. I love you so much. I'm so thankful and blessed to have shared all this time with you in my life. You have been such a good Mom. I'm just so sorry that this last year was a bad year for me with my Fibromyalgia. I feel like it robbed a year of my life with you, had I known."

Tears welled up in my eyes. I didn't mean to cry in front of her. My feelings were just so raw.

I wiped my eyes and said I would go make us a yummy cup of coffee. Mom told me she would be out in a little bit. I smiled at her, picked up the food tray and went in the kitchen to make us a cup of coffee. She soon got up and we sat outside in the patio and shared Saturday morning coffee in the sunshine. It was a beautiful day. The skies were so blue and the birds were chirping. A lovely Spring day for my Mom. We talked about Marylou coming out for a short visit at lunchtime. This made her happy. She said,

"It is so sweet of Angie to pick her up."

I replied back, "Yes. She is a very sweet friend and she knows what a special friendship you and Marylou have."

She went in her room to get ready and I was straightening up the house for our company when my telephone rang. I answered the phone and it was Susan from Hospice. She said the she received the referral for my Mom, Marybeth, and would like to come out this weekend if that was possible? I said, yes of course. I thought to myself, "Wow. That was a fast referral!" We made an appointment for later Saturday afternoon. I went upstairs to share the news with my husband. We were thankful for the care that Mom was going to get. We decided to not tell Mom yet and let her enjoy her day with her best friend.

Angie and Marylou arrived promptly at 11:00. Mom and Marylou hugged tightly. I privately thanked Angie and told her much this means to all of us. I made coffees for the two M & M's, they sat outside for a lovely visit. Angie and I went in the house and we sat and had a cup of coffee together as the soup heated up. I had set the table for the two M & M's, with my special place settings, flowers and candles. I wanted them to have a nice lunch together. I asked Angie if she was hungry and she had a late breakfast. The two best friends shared lunch, laughter and stories with each other. After lunch I could see my Mom was getting tired and asked if she wanted to rest on the sofa. She said yes that sounds like a good idea. If my Mom wasn't sick, she would have been as full of energy just like Marylou. Sadly, there was an obvious difference in my Mom now.

We confirmed our Barona Casino plans for two Sundays from this weekend. The M & M's hugged and said their goodbyes. I thanked Angie again and said I would see her on Monday at work. After they left I asked Mom if she wanted to rest in the living room or in her room? She opted for her bedroom.

I told her that the case worker from Hospice called and she would come out later this afternoon. She agreed with me how fast they were taking care of her, but in the back of my mind, I was silently freaking out that Mom would be in Hospice. I knew if I had these feelings, surely my Mom did too, so I offered comforting words. I said, "Mama. I know this is all scary and hearing the word Hospice is alarming. It just means you are going to get *amazing* care from them. You never have to go to some other place if you don't want to. This is your home and if you want to be at home, then you will be here."

You could see relief in her eyes as she sat on her bed, then she replied, "I want to be at home." I smiled at her and reached out to her frail hand and assured her that I will make sure of that. I told her I loved her and would see her later. I went upstairs, emotionally exhausted. I turned my fan on and lay on my bed staring at the ceiling. The sound of the fan soon put me to sleep. I took a much needed short nap while my Mom did too. Since returning from New York, up to this day, it had been non-stop busy. Go, go, go, hospital, hospital, go, go, go, cancer, cancer! Dammit, Dammit!

I woke up an hour later and went to check on Mom and check her pain level. It was time for her pain medicine and this time she asked for them. I knew her pain was beginning to get worse for her. I would have to ask if she needed pain medicine before, and now she was starting to ask me for them. Since the day after she came home from being admitted in the hospital a week ago, today, she seemed a bit different. She was very tired, more than normal. I also thought , *maybe the short visit with Marylou took a little wind out of her sail?*

Having never experienced Hospice, first hand, I really didn't know what to expect, but I would find out soon. My telephone rang, it was Susan and she was trying to find our condo, so I directed her to us. I invited Susan in and went to let Mom know she was here. I helped her up and out into the living room. The three of us sat on the sofa as Susan introduced herself and began to explain what Hospice will offer regarding care. Mom's oncologist would be her doctor going forward. There would be a case nurse assigned to my Mom who would come out as often as needed and who would report to her oncologist and that Susan would be her case worker.

The process of being admitted as a Hospice patient means that the patient has six months or less to live. The patient does not need to go to the hospital any more. Since the doctors knew what Mom's medical diagnosis was, all of her care would be in her own home. The reason to go to a Hospice facility would be for a number of reasons, such as there is no other caregiver at home with the patient or if pain control could no longer be managed at home, they would need to go to a Hospice care facility. Also, if it was the wish of the patient was to not be at home when they are close to passing away, they can request to go to the facility. Some people do choose that.

Hospice would be there not only to help the patient, but to help the family as well. They are available twenty-four hours a day for questions, concerns or requests needed. Medicare would pay for all costs for Hospice including any comfort medications needed, a hospital bed, a wheelchair, a walker, a shower chair, oxygen, any medical items that would help make the patient comfortable. Her medications would be delivered to our home as needed, also twenty-four hours a day.

As Susan explained all of the options of care for my Mom, we both felt more at ease. Mom would have a health aide to come out and help her with self-care, preparing meals or cleaning if needed. There would someone to offer healing light massage and even Reiki therapy if desired. There are Chaplains available for comfort if Mom was religious, which was very nice to know. They had volunteers who would come make videos of her if she wished or volunteers to help her with any projects she felt she needed to complete before she said her last goodbye. The list of care and volunteers was amazing.

This initial appoint took about two hours to complete. Going through Mom's medical background, current medications and vitamins, her religious preferences and a physical exam of blood pressure, oxygen check, questions on her current pain and what symptoms she has been having. It was a very thorough appointment. The reason for it, was to determine all the care she would need or want. As her illness would progress, her needs would be reassessed.

I explained to Susan that my husband Ron and I would be her main caregivers and between our work schedules and the nurses or health aides that would come to the house, we would attempt to never have Mom alone. I also voiced for my Mom that she did not want to go to a Hospice facility and she desired to be at home through this journey. Susan noted all this down.

Susan asked specifically about a Living Will (the Advanced Care Directive), I explained we had worked on that and her Will, we just needed to finalize it with witnesses and a Notary. Susan explained the importance of the Advanced Care Directive, so that my Mom's wishes would be met regarding any resuscitation in the event her heart stopped or something of that nature. My Mom spoke up, "I know I don't want to be kept alive on machines. I want to go if it's my time." As difficult as that was to hear, I had to support Mom's wishes.

At this point another, "Do Not Resuscitate", had to be filled out on a Hospice form stating what she wanted or didn't want. Susan explained that she would be kept out of pain and discomfort as the cancer progressed. Susan then discussed the on-going use of my Mom's current medications which three of her medications where Lisinopril for blood pressure, Plavix for her Coronary Artery Disease, and Lipitor for her cholesterol. As we were talking, Susan was typing on her laptop entering in the information. She listed all of my Mom's medicines and told us which ones were considered comfort medications and it would be my Mom's choice to continue taking her other medicines and vitamins.

Plavix and Lipitor were not on the Hospice Medications, but Mom was welcome to still fill them at her regular pharmacy if she wished to continue taking them. My Mom said, "Oh yes, I want to keep taking them." I replied, "No problem Mama. I will make sure you get them." Susan said, "Okay. I will order the care package of Hospice medications. They will be delivered in a couple of hours. Some of them you may use and some you may not need. We just want you to be prepared, just in case." She began reading the list of medications and explained what they were for. These are the following medications that my Mom would receive:

Acetaminophen 650mg. suppository for pain and temperature, if needed

Temazepam 15mg. capsules for insomnia

Morphine Sulfate 20mg – liquid to take every two hours for pain and if shortness of breath occurs

Senna Plus tablet for constipation as needed

Prochlorperazine 10mg tablet, use for nausea every six hours

Bisacodyl 10mg suppository as needed for constipation

Prochlorperazine 25mg suppository as needed for nausea/vomiting every six hours

Atropine Sulfate Opthalmatic 1% oral solution every four hours as needed

for moderate to severe secretions

Lorazepam 0.5mg every four hours for mild anxiety, restlessness and shortness of breath

Oxygen 2-4 liters per minute, as needed using comfort Nasal Cannula

When Susan completed reading these medicines, she asked if we had any questions. My Mom asked,

"Do I have to take the Morphine? I don't want to be out of it?" I spoke and said

"Mama, you don't have to take it if you don't want it. It will be here in case your pain gets out of control. Remember how rested you felt in the hospital, once you weren't being poked and prodded like a pin cushion? The hospital had you on Morphine for pain control. I can assure you Mama, I understand you want to be coherent for as long as possible. I want you to be too. But I don't want you to feel like you need to suffer if the cancer is hurting you. I will be your voice when you can't speak. I will honor your wishes and I will take care of you. I love you."

I held her hand for comfort.

Susan agreed with me and gently explained the medications and the usage, which seemed to ease my Mom some. Nothing about this appointment was anything I thought I would ever need to know about or my Mom either. Who wants to think, *I want terminal stage four cancer and Hospice please.* Being admitted into Hospice really marks the beginning of the final journey and there is well-deserved fear of the unknown. Being a Hospice patient does allow an enormous amount of care that you wouldn't otherwise see. Compassion, empathy and the support is priceless. If your own family is traveling on this journey and Hospice is suggested, I highly recommend considering it, accepting it and allowing the beautiful comfort it will bring. Pride can stop some families for accepting Hospice, or their religious background and upbringing could not seek the help. Think of the caring people of Hospice as *Angels with skin.*

Susan asked to see Mom's bedroom and bathroom to assess her physical needs. Mom's bedroom was on the first floor and her bathroom was right next to her bedroom. My husband and I had already installed handrails in the shower and a shower seat with handles, to help my Mom, if she was weak. Hospice would have helped with these items, but we had already been proactive.

Mom's bedroom was quaint. This was the second largest bedroom in our townhouse. I hung new curtains for her that matched her duvet, pretty like Springtime, her favorite season. She had a dresser and her flat screen TV, a nightstand and an antique vanity. Pictures of her family dotted the shelves. Susan rejoined my Mom and I on the sofa and mentioned that as the illness progresses getting up and around may be more difficult.

They could deliver a hospital bed that would adjust up and down to help my Mom, when the time came for the need of it.

She said the bedroom had an awkward right angle going into the bedroom and the hospital bed may not be able to fit into the angle of the room. I told Susan that we had discussed this briefly and if the time came where my Mom needed the hospital bed, we could use the space between the living room and the dining room and I would move all the furniture needed. We wanted to do anything to make Mom comfortable. She said that many families do this to accommodate their loved and helps to keep their ill family member feeling still as part of the family. Mom agreed this would be fine with her.

The next part of the appointment would be ordering the care items that Mom would need. A portable oxygen tank was ordered along with the oxygen room tank. A light weight wheelchair, a bed stand on wheels, like used at hospitals was ordered. She said that so many more things are available and we can talk to her case nurse as the illness progresses and the medical needs change.

Our appointment was winding down and I could see Mom was physically and emotionally wiped out. Susan handed us each a card to call if we need anything and she handed a packet of papers for signatures. Once this was done, we were given a Hospice care folder which contained copies of all of this information and a couple pamphlets about Hospice and what to expect. I shook her hand and we said our good-byes.

I looked over at my Mom said, "Well, you will be well taken care of." I placed my hand on her frail thin hands that were covered in the deep purple spots and smiled at her. She looked at me and replied,

"This is not how I pictured this would be Ronda, but it is what it is."

I asked her, "Do you want some soup?"

"No thanks honey. Just a drink and some pain meds please," she said.

"Do you want a margarita or a pina colada?" I asked her.

She laughed and said, "Oh a pina colada later!"

So I got her a drink and her medicines. She said she was going to go take a nap. I said enjoy your nap and I will wake you for dinner if you are up to it.

I was surprised at how fast the medicines were delivered for my Mom. They arrived in less than an hour. I signed for them and compared the medications to the list we should have. They were all here. There was one that stated it needed to be refrigerated and that was the Atropine Sulfate drops. I went and placed them on the door if the refrigerator.

My husband was getting ready for work and he made a light dinner for everyone. We all sat at the dinner table together and enjoyed a nice family dinner. Mom had an appetite, which was wonderful. After Ron left for work, Mom and I sat in the patio. We really have a lovely view of our short rocky mountains and Mom commented on them and how much she loves this season.

That evening we watched a "teary, feel-good girl movie", like we did when I was a teenager. A box of Kleenex between us and a sappy girl movie, how perfect! After our movie I asked her if she needed anything other than her medicines, and she said no she was fine. She got settled in bed, I kissed her good night and wished her sweet dreams. I went upstairs and collapsed on my bed.

Sunday, April 1st. I woke up and went downstairs to check on Mom. She was just waking up. I asked her if she wanted to shower this morning. She said no, she wasn't up to a shower today. I was a bit concerned, having grown up with my

Mom's vanity, I needed to understand she just didn't feel well and accept the changes. I said,

"Okay. I will make coffee so when you feel like getting up I will pour you a cup. How is your pain level?"

"Well, it was starting to hurt, so I already got up and took two pain pills right about 6:00a.m."

"Okay Mama. I will see you when you feel like getting up."

I walked in the kitchen made some coffee for me and soon she was up, so I poured her a cup as well. Coffee the miracle elixir for her. I know that wonderful smell of fresh brewed coffee would get her up and it gave me a little bit of relief that she still wanted to drink coffee.

    We sat out on the patio relishing in the glorious Spring morning. I knew she really enjoyed this beauty. We talked about her visit with Marylou yesterday. That visit really brightened her spirits. Mom asked me to thank Angie again for her help to get Marylou to our house. I said I would. Ron woke up and we discussed how the appointment went yesterday. I told him that the medical care items would be delivered this morning. He was impressed with the service Mom was getting too.

    I suggested we run to the store to pick up the groceries to make a nice Sunday dinner. I let my Michael know we would be leaving for about thirty minutes and would be right back. I gave Susan my cell number yesterday for all calls to come to this number rather than the home number, in case Mom was resting and items would be delivered. My Mom went to rest while we went down to the store.

    Ron and I dashed down to the grocery store. We picked up the items to make stuffed cabbage that was Marylou's recipe. Mom loved this. I couldn't think of a better comfort food. We got back and I had time to prepare the stuffed cabbage and to slow cook it for about three hours in my giant pot that was a gift from Marylou. She knew we had such a big family and that we loved to cook.

My cell phone rang and it was the deliveryman from the medical supply company. He confirmed our address and said he would arrive in about fifteen minutes. Then my phone rang again and the caller ID came up as Hospice. I had programmed the phone number in on Saturday into my cell phone, because I knew I would need this number. I answered the phone and said,

"Hello. This is Ronda."

The woman on the other end replied, "Hello Ronda. My name is Marie. I am the case nurse for your Mom, Marybeth."

"Wow, thank you that was fast. I really appreciate that."

We chatted for a few minutes and she wanted to come out today for the initial visit and meet my Mom. She asked "What time would be good to stop in?" I told her anytime as we would be home for the rest of the day. She said she could come now. I provided her directions for our condo and we hung up the phone. I heard the delivery truck out back of my home and walked outside.

I greeted the delivery man and showed him into our home. He unloaded the wheelchair and bed table. When he brought in the oxygen tanks and the house oxygen machine, he said he would like to set it up and show us how to properly use it. I knocked on Mom's door and let her know the oxygen was here. She said we could come in and the man set up the tank and showed us how to measure the oxygen and where to pour in the distilled water. He gave Mom both an eight ft. Nasal Canella and on that was fifty ft., so she could be very mobile. He also provided the portable tanks, so she could take it anywhere and in case there was a power outage. He gave us "Oxygen in Use" signs to stick on our outside windows too.

We thanked him and he left. Mom seemed to be more comfortable with the oxygen and I felt better that she finally had it. We were all surprised that they hadn't originally sent her home with oxygen, but that is Medicare. She asked for some pain medicine, so I went and got her some. I asked her if she was hungry and she said yes. This was good news to hear.

I got Mom settled on the couch when my cell phone rang again. It was Marie, the nurse and she wanted to know where to park? I directed her to our visitor parking spaces and let her know I would meet her out back of my condo. Up walked a friendly woman wheeling a bag behind her. I introduced myself and we shook hands. I let her know my Mom was up from a nap so this was really good timing. We went inside my home. I smiled at Mom when we walked inside she smiled back at me. I said, "Look who I found."

Marie the nurse introduced herself to my Mom and began with her own background and what she will do to care for her. She discussed all the assorted care options and volunteers that were available to help. She then began to ask my Mom her current symptoms and a brief history of her illness. She apologized that it was almost duplicate information, but this would help her with my Mom's care.

I helped to answer some of the more emotionally difficult questions, so my Mom didn't have to. Having to discuss the cancer was a hard subject and I was going to help her in any way I could. Obviously, Mom said what she needed to and she did allow me to answer, on her behalf, of what led her to the Hospital, the diagnosis and now to Hospice. We both liked this nurse. She was very kind and compassionate. To do the job she does on a day to day basis, takes a very special person.

We went over the current medications both from Mom's primary doctor and from Hospice. She explained to Mom about the medicines and explained to both of us the importance of pain control. If we could manage the pain here at home then she would have her wishes to remain at home during this illness. She explained the use of the oxygen. It would be ideal that Mom use it while sleeping and if it makes her more comfortable she can use it in the day.

Marie asked my Mom if the Norco was taking away her pain. "Well it does help, I just have to be very regular now," she answered. The Norco had been prescribed when she left the hospital. At first she wasn't asking for the pain medicine and I would have to ask her if she was in pain, so she would take it and get some relief. I shared this with the nurse and my concern if it wasn't going to continue relieving her pain. Marie explained the liquid Morphine that Hospice provided would help take the pain. Because it was a liquid even just a few drops would help right away and could be used between the time period to take the Norco.

Mom spoke up and she said she didn't want to take the Morphine. She was very adamant about not taking it. I looked in her eyes as she spoke. I felt that she was saying this out of fear. Fear from being too out of it from the Morphine. Marie told her that the amount that was being suggested to use, would not make her loopy. She would still be coherent and would be able to function with pain relief.

I reassured Mom again, I would not make her take something she didn't want to and softly reminded her that she should not need to suffer in pain over fear of not being able to participate in life. I understood the fears she had. I myself was given way too much Morphine after my son Michael was born from an emergency c section. I wasn't coherent all day and couldn't even hold my new baby until that evening. My Mom was at the hospital with me that day and maybe she remembered how I was.

Mom had been very fortunate in her life to have relatively a healthy life. No major surgeries other than child birth. So she didn't have much personal medical history to draw from other than in the more recent years with the coronary artery disease and her stroke a year and a half earlier. I tried to ease her fear of this unknown, so did her nurse.

Marie said that she could also call in a stronger pain medicine if the Norco was not working. The timeline was having four hours of pain relief. If her pain was spiking sooner than that, to call the Hospice phone number and they would page her or the on call nurse, if Marie was off work. She explained that the Hospice phone number was available twenty-four hours a day and that we could call anytime we needed. Also the pharmacy delivered twenty-four hours a day.

The next part of this visit would be a physical exam and to take her vitals and oxygen saturation levels. At this point I excused myself so she could have some privacy and I went into the kitchen and heated up some potato soup and made a plate with crackers and cut up cantaloupe. I poured half of the chocolate nutrition drink in a cup and set the dining room table for my Mom. She still wanted to have some normalcy in her life. She always ate at the table. Even in her illness, she still wanted this too. This was fine with me, anything to make her feel good.

Marie said she was done with her exam and would report to the oncologist and also would recommend a health aide during the week to help with showering and preparing lunches. I explained to Marie my work schedule and my husband's work schedules. Marie was going to do her best to work within our schedules so that Mom would not have to be alone for too long. This was a relief to all of us. Her nurse would call daily and would come in at least a few times a week or more if needed. We thanked her and she left. Mom commented on how much she liked her and I had to agree. She was a very nice person.

I helped Mom up to the table and got her set. I was happy to see that she had an appetite. This gave me hope that she was doing okay considering everything. Ron came downstairs and we went out on our patio so I could let him know what would go on and the care for Mom. It relieved us both. Mom joined us outside and we talked and shared a few stories. We all agreed that it was a coincidence that Mom's nurse had a name that started with an M. I told her that was a good sign. She smiled.

I could see that she had some discomfort so I asked her she wanted to go inside and I could bring the oxygen in the living room? She said thank you but she was going to go rest. I followed her to her bedroom and helped her get settled with the oxygen canella. She seemed a bit more at ease and it made me very aware that she could not be off the oxygen too long. I wished her sweet dreams and that we would have a nice family Sunday dinner later. She blew me a kiss and smiled at me.

Ron and I went upstairs and laid on the bed talking about everything. I started crying and he held me tight. The tears just wouldn't stop. There just were no words that could be said at this moment. Nothing could make this situation better. All I wanted was my Mom to be cancer free, but that wish was not going to be granted. I fell asleep for a bit, which was greatly needed. It is important that the caregivers get rest too.

I got up and Ron and I went downstairs to get dinner set. I went into my Mom's room to check on her and her pain. I gently spoke and asked if she wanted to come out for a Sunday Dinner? She said yes, but asked to sit on the couch. I said, "No problem Mama. Whatever you want. I will get the dinner tray for you."

The four of us had a lovely dinner and my Mom surprised us all by eating two pieces of stuffed cabbage! She said she was so hungry, which made us all feel better. Her appetite had diminished so much lately, so it made me feel better to see her eat. She had become so thin and so frail looking in the last month especially. I mentioned I was going to call Auntie M later and find out if she was going to come down for a visit now. This made her happy. After dinner I made us all a nice cup of coffee.

Mom had been up for less than an hour and she said she was going to go rest and now that her tummy was full from dinner. I helped her with her oxygen and got her settled in her room. I asked if she wanted to watch any TV and she said sure. She hadn't been too interested in it either, so this was also a sign for me she was feeling better. I asked her to call me if she needed anything.

I went upstairs to call my Auntie M. I told her how the Hospice admission went we met Hospice nurse Mary today. Auntie M said to me, "Oh honey, the people of Hospice are Angels with skin. They will help you take good care of your Mom. I talked to Uncle Glen about coming down before we go to our house in St. Thomas, and I decided to come down this week. I want to come down and laugh with my sister, paint her toes, do her hair and just come play with my big Sissy." I said how happy this would make Mom. She was thinking of coming Wednesday or Thursday and would let us know tomorrow.

Auntie had also talked to their brother, my Uncle J, and he said he was planning on coming the following week. I said this would be good to stagger visits for Mom's sake. I explained how much Mom is sleeping now from a week ago and that it seems like every day, she sleeps more and more. To the point of she is almost asleep now more than she is awake. I did say that she had an appetite today and ate well.

Auntie told me this is just part of it. She had personally lost four dear people including her best friend in the past year to cancer. We both agreed that cancer is the "B" word that rhymes with witch! (I'm trying to be polite) She said that she was looking forward to this visit and she just had to come see Mom now and she wanted to help give Ron and I a break. She also said we won't go through this alone and she will come back in another month or two, to help as Mom progresses. I thanked her and told her how much I appreciate that.

Auntie also told me during this phone conversation a very useful tip, and that was if *anyone* offers help to say, "Yes please." She said if they wanted to run an errand, bring a casserole, anything that could help, to accept the help. This will be a long emotionally and physically draining process. Having always taken care of my family or to have been the friend to help others, this would be a different role I would need to accept. I knew I would need to. Trying to maintain a career, juggling care of my sweet Mama and to stay positive and sunny, in what would soon become some of my darkest days. I knew I would need help emotionally, physically and spiritually.

    Most of us are very prideful people. Raised to take care of yourself and your families. A very big part of this journey is to be able to *know* when to accept help that is offered. You must put aside your pride and accept the help from family members, friends, co-workers, neighbors and the Angels of Hospice. This can be a long, difficult journey for the whole family, so any help can make a huge difference and is very appreciated!

    On Monday morning I woke up a little more rested. Took a shower, got ready and went down to give medicines to my Mom. She had already been awake and said she got up for some pain pills. I acted calm and said okay.

"Do you want me to fix something to eat before I go to work?"

She said, "No. I will get some toast later."

I also shared the good news of Auntie M coming for a visit this week. I suggested she give her a call later and find out when she was scheduled to fly in. We laughed when I told her that she wanted to come play with her big Sissy. I hugged and kissed her goodbye and then went to wake up my son Michael to get ready for school.

    This week we had training for our new accounting software at my office. As I trained all week, I knew I would be juggling between work and caring for my Mom. I was no stranger to illness and a career, but this was entirely a new path in life. One I didn't want to be on. A path that would not lead to a happy place, at least for me. I was not ready to *not* have my Mom in my life. This weighed heaving on my heart and soul.

I arrived at work at immediately dove into all the tasks I could take on before training started at 8:00 a.m. Working was actually a bit of comfort for me because when I was at work, I was very busy as a Contracts Administrator for a construction company. I had no time to think about anything else, which was a blessing. However, I knew that Hospice was going to call me today, so it did pop in my thoughts occasionally.

The health aide called me to schedule her visit for today. I told her the time my Mom seemed to be awake and we scheduled it for about 10:30 a.m. I called my Mom on her cell. "Hello Sweetie," she answered. Her voice sounded so good to my ears. She sounded like her normal self and that brought me comfort. I let her know about her health aide coming out at 10:30 and that I would be home about 11:30. Before I hung up the phone, I asked her if she wanted or needed anything before I came home. She said no.

When I got home my Mom was showered and in fresh clothes. She was resting on the couch and seemed well. My husband Ron had just arrived home from his first job, this was perfect timing. I hugged and kissed him and we made lunch. I grabbed mine to go and I hugged my Mom and said I would see her after work.

I returned to my office for the afternoon training. The day zipped by. I drove home and Ron was in the kitchen preparing dinner for all of us, which was so nice. I was very happy to see Mom awake and sitting in the patio in her favorite chair and having a cup of coffee and her cigarette. Our whole family said that if she wanted to keep smoking, to let her. It couldn't do anymore harm. This seemed to keep her calmer too. I had noticed though, she was barely smoking. Maybe it was how ill she felt, or the pressure on her lungs from fluid? But I had noticed how little she smoked.

I asked her how she was feeling and she said she felt good. She went and took a nap after the lunch. She had a full belly and a wonderful nap. She was cheerful and seemed happy. To see this normal side of my Mom, was a blessing. She seemed like herself again. I thought to myself, *Maybe she had been so sick from pneumonia and the fluid on her lungs, that maybe she's going to be okay for a while*? I would treasure anytime I would have with her.

My darling husband made my Mom and I our coffees and brought them to us. He wanted to pamper his favorite ladies and smiled at both of us. He was so good to our family and loved my Mom. He had moved from New York a year and a half ago to start a life with me and my family. He knew we were a package deal. My Mom adored him and was so happy we found each other. She told me that he is my real life Angel. I smiled and agreed. She said

"I am so happy he is here for you."

"Me too Mama. I don't know how I would get through this without him. He loves you too."

"I know honey and I love him back", she replied.

It was a magnificent Monday evening. With Spring flowers blooming, from our home you could smell the Jasmine and Magnolia Flowers. Such a sweet smell filled the air, a gentle breeze flowing by and all the beautiful little birds flying around and chirping. My Mom loved everything about Spring and this was just a perfect evening of enjoyment with a wonderful afternoon cup of coffee together under the blue skies.

Soon dinner was done and we all sat at the dining room table and shared a nice light dinner together, my Mom, myself, Ron and Michael. We talked and laughed about silly stories of past. It was so nice to just have a small bit of time that was not about the cancer, but about being a family, loving and laughing. I couldn't ask for more, and I was thankful.

Ron had to leave for his next job, he hugged and kissed everyone then he left for work. I went and got the oxygen machine for the living room that way Mom could visit. I got her settled and comfortable on the sofa with her down comforter we gave her at Christmas. She loved this fluffy comforter because it made her feel so cozy. It was nice to have her relax and just be.

I went and got her medicine trays to fill up her vitamins and medicines she needs for mornings or evenings during the next week. We sat together on the sofa and watch her favorite show, *The Big Bang Theory*, and she directed me to her night meds and morning meds. She still wanted all her other medicines that her primary doctor had prescribed and now added are the sleeping medicine, the anxiety meds, nausea meds and the pain meds. I gave her a drink and her night medicines, I asked her if she can let me know when the pain medicines feel like they are wearing off, so if they aren't strong enough, the pharmacy can change it. She said she was okay tonight, this was good.

Both of my daughters were bringing their kids over to visit with their Oma. All of them loved her so much. For Brendon, my three year old grandson, Oma was his favorite person in the entire world. Oma and he spent so much time together since he was born. Jake and Josh loved Oma so much too. It was bittersweet when they came by. All of us grownups knew the finality of what we we're facing but these three little boys had no idea that Oma was dying, they just knew she was sick.

This evening was April 2nd. It was my daughter Addie's birthday. Since the night I took my Mom to the Urgent Care on March 15th, everyday seemed to just blend together into the next. Birthdays in our home were *always* celebrated. We all treasured life and the family in it. Birthdays were special, except this birthday for Addie, was postponed in celebration, because Grandma was so sick. On this evening we were just all grateful to be together.

All the boys went to Oma with big giant smiles on their faces to see her. They were like three little suns to brighten her evening with love and smiles. Oma looked at them and smiled. Each of them climbed up very carefully and gave her a big hug and kiss. I watched this love and had to fight the tears back. I thought, *How are they going to handle their Oma going away to be an Angel*? My daughters were visibly choked up too. After they visited for a little bit I corralled the kids out in the patio and gave them some cookies and drinks. My daughters stayed in with their Grandma to have a visit with her.

We laughed and shared some good times that evening. She told us about her sister coming down on Thursday and she was so excited. After a nice visit, she said she was tired and wanted to go to her room. I said, "No problem Mama, I will help get you settled." I brought the oxygen machine in for her and she lay down on the bed. I asked her if she wanted to get in pajamas. She said no I'm fine in my leggings and t-shirt. I went in the living room and got her comforter and pillows, then went and tucked her in. I reminded her to call me on my cell phone and I will be down for anything at any time she needs me. We laughed that our cell phones became our new intercom system, because I wouldn't hear her call me if I were upstairs in my bedroom, so this worked great. I gave my girls a big hug and my grandsons too. We all said are goodbyes.

After they left I hopped in a quick shower and laid in bed thinking about everything happening. The tears started flowing again. This was a nightly experience now. It was hard to get it wrapped around *my* head that she is so very sick. I see her eat. I see her drink coffee. We talk and laugh and she even wanted to watch her favorite TV show. She's beautiful and has her sense of humor, but she is terminally ill with months to live, so the oncologist says. I prayed that night for strength for my Mom and to take her fear away. I prayed for comfort and peace for her.

The next morning, it was the regular schedule as usual. I got up, made coffee, jumped in the shower, got my hair and makeup done and then dressed for the office. I went downstairs and gently knocked on my Mom's door and went in her room. All you could hear was the oxygen machine sucking in the ambient air and swooshing out in a continuous and rhythmic sound. I didn't want to wake her but I was afraid to let her get into pain by not taking her medicine.

I walked over to her bed and she opened her eyes. I said,

"Good morning sunshine."

She said, "Good morning sweetie."

I asked if she would like her medicines before I left for work. She said without hesitation, "Yes please." I asked how her pain was and she said about a six or seven. I gave her the medicine and a drink. I also placed some crackers and applesauce on her tray stand, in case she got hungry.

"Mama, your aide Winnie is coming today around 9:00am. She will help you get showered and changed in fresh clothes. I told her to come on in the house, in case you are sleeping when she gets here." Mom said okay. I also asked her if she would call me when she feels the pain coming on stronger again so I can help keep track of it. Marie the nurse had explained for me to watch this and her pain started back up in 3-4 hours that Mom had two options, one was to use a few drops of the liquid Morphine and the other was to get a stronger pain pill.

I hugged and kissed her goodbye and told her I would be home for lunch. I went and woke up my son for school. Ron walked me out to my car, as he does every morning for work. We hugged a little tighter, we exchanged loving words and we said we would see each other later. I drove into my office and was gearing myself up for the work day and training that lay ahead.

I went into training at 7:00 am until 8:30 am., then would be back in later in the afternoon. This allowed me time to call and check on Mom. I also received a call on my cell phone about 10:30 from Marie the nurse. She asked me how Mom was doing. I explained that she seems to be in more pain and the medicine seems to wear off by three to four hours. She knew how my Mom felt about the morphine, but she was trying to encourage the use of just a couple drops. This would be enough to get the pain tolerable. I told her I was going home at lunch and would ask her. Marie asked if she could stop by later to check on her. I said "Of course you can. That would make her feel better too."

I finished some business tasks and then left for lunch about 11:30. I drove home and Mom was sitting in the patio without her oxygen. She smiled when I walked in and she said, "Oh honey, I love Winnie. She is such a beautiful woman. She's married and has five kids and six grandchildren. Oh, I *feel* so much better!" There is nothing like how a shower not only cleanses the body, it can cleanse one's soul too, especially if you have been ill.

Mom went on to tell me she loves her haircut and loves the chestnut color I had dyed her hair. "Mama, I will keep coloring your hair for you and can assure you that you won't have gray roots!" We both laughed at her vanity. I went into the kitchen to heat up some vegetable barley soup and popped in a piece of bread in the toaster for her. I asked her if she wanted to eat lunch outside or in the dining room? She said she would love to stay in the patio because it's such a beautiful day.

It was so good to see my Mom have a bit more pep in her step. This is the most I have seen her up for any length in a while. I told her that nurse Marie would be stopping in later. She wanted to check on you and the pain control. I shared the phone conversation that Marie and I had this morning about the use of the Morphine. I gently said that you might consider a couple drops if after two hours of taking the other pain pills and your pain spikes, it will help. She also might order a bit stronger pain pill too.

After lunch, Mom said she wanted to go lay down in her room. I helped her up, as her strength wasn't there. We went inside and walked down the hall to her bedroom. She immediately walked to her oxygen machine and put the nasal cannula on. She sat on the edge of the bed catching her breath, and then was able to get her breathing rhythm back. She lay back into her mound of plushy pillows. I laughed and said, "You are a Queen! Look at all your pillows. I wish I could stay and lay there, but I have to go do more training." She smiled and wished me a nice day.

I gave her the next round of medicine and got her settled. I placed her remote for her TV, in easy reach, in case she wanted to watch a movie or something. I gave her a kiss on her cheek and said I would see her soon. My husband was home now, so I filled him in on the details of her shower, her lunch, which she only ate about half a cup of soup and one bite of toast. I also let Ron know that nurse Marie would be coming out this afternoon after her other patient. She might change Mom's pain medicines.

I returned to work and training for the day, which seemed to zip on by. When I arrived home her nurse was just about to leave. I was glad that I caught her after my Mom's visit. Their visit was done in Mom's bedroom that afternoon. She never got back up for the day. Marie the nurse asked me how Mom's sleeping was. I told her that I am starting to notice that she seems to sleep more and more, to the point she is asleep more than she's awake. I also mentioned her increased pain level.

Marie told me that this is part of the illness. The pain does increase as does the sleep. She said she has already consulted with her oncologist and he agreed to order a stronger pain medicine. Again, Marie talked to me about the liquid Morphine. I assured her if I could see my Mom in more pain, I will suggest using a couple drops to see if it helps? None of us wanted her to suffer, least of all herself. Marie said she would stop by in the morning, if that was okay? I said of course, anytime. She called in the pharmacy for Percocet's and told me they would be delivered within a couple hours.

A little while later, we heard a car drive up and it was the pharmacy. The man knocked on our door and I went to answer it. He had me sign the delivery slip and I thanked him for coming out. I immediately went to my Mom's room and let her know her new pain medicines had arrived. She was allowed to take 2 at a time. I gave her the option of one or two pills and she said, "Two please." I mentioned she needs to take this with some food or her nutrition drink and she just wanted the drink.

I brought up the use of the liquid Morphine as an option. She looked at me with her beautiful brown eyes and I could see the fear again. I sat on her bed and told her that I would never make her take it, but if the pain continues to get worse before four hours that she should try just a couple drops. It is enough to help the pain surge in between the next pain medicine dose and it was not enough to make her loopy. I also mentioned that if her breathing became strained, even with the use of oxygen, the Morphine will help calm her breathing. I wished her sweet dreams, gave her a kiss on the cheek.

CHAPTER 5 - THE SIGNS

The signs that a person will have when they get closer to walking their final journey of life will vary from each person. This will depend on the type of cancer, as each may have unique signs, while there are many similar processes a person will go through. The oncologist doctor would be your first person to ask and he/she may be able to direct you to medical websites for accurate descriptions if you need them. For my Mom, she had an aggressive non-small cell lung cancer, adenocarcinoma. Her journey began many months prior, only we had no idea she was ill.

There will be a beginning of disinterest in things that were once normal things for your loved one to do or enjoy. Maybe they enjoyed Music or certain TV programs and now have no interest in it at all? They will slowly stop wanting to go to their favorite places. Food and drink become the very apparent signs that the illness is progressing. When normal eating or drinking lessons. I would recommend for the caretaker to pay close attention to this aspect as the final journey is underway. The sleeping is already happening. Sleeping time will take over the day and being awake will lesson. This becomes the new normal.

Sleeping helps them on their journey they will board in the next few months. We are raised when you are sick, make chicken noodle soup to feel better and keep your body nourished. Eating and sharing meals, like families had done together with special celebrations, holidays and birthday parties and just simple dinners, food and drink are a part of life. When you start to see your loved one begin a disinterest in their favorite foods and beverages, when you see how little your loved one eats or drinks at all, this is harder for the family to cope with than the patient. The thought that food will keep you well, in this situation, must be placed on some imaginary shelf and take the queues from their *not* wanting to eat or drink. Allow them to decide, they know what their body and soul needs.

Wednesday, April 4th, her signs were apparent today. The day started like the rest of the week. Waking, getting ready for work, checking on Mom for her pain and to offer her food and drink. She seemed great this morning. Cheerful and happy her sister was coming tomorrow. She took her pain medicines and drank a few sips of the nutrition drink. I kissed her goodbye and told her that I would stop in for an early lunch about 10:00a.m.

I drove to work and dove immediately to emails and items I needed to process before the training started at 8:00am. I went through the training and I then I called Mom when I was done. She sounded so good on the phone. Her voice sounded like my cheerful, sweet Mama. She gave me hope she was doing okay. I asked her if she wanted anything before I came home and she said no.

I drove home and made some coffee and asked her if she would like a cup? She said, "No honey, I have my water." I didn't think it was anything at the time, her not wanting coffee. We talked about her conversation with her sissy coming to visit her tomorrow and how excited she was. I smiled and I was happy too. I asked her if I could make her a snack or some soup. She said, no thanks, she was just not hungry. It was just about time for me to leave back to work and I told her Ron would be home in 20 minutes.

She said, "I'll be fine sweetie. I'm just going to enjoy the quiet." I smiled at her and said, "You do that Mama. You deserve some peace." I gave her a hug and kiss. "I'll be home later", I said, as I walked out into the patio to leave. I got into my car and had to fight back my tears. The emotions definitely come and go, and this was one of the moments. I took a few deep breaths and started my car and drove into work.

I finished my main training today at my office, which was good. I would have one final session tomorrow. *Yippee*! I thought. I called my Mom before I left the office to come home and find out if she wanted anything like chocolate cake, ice cream or margaritas? No, nothing sounded appealing to her. I will see you shortly. I drove home and she was sitting outside in the patio on her favorite chair. She smiled as I walked in and I smiled back.

"Mama, how are you feeling now?"

She smiled at me, "Honey, I feel good. I've had a lot of rest. I was hungry and I ate my whole bowl of soup today."

"That's great Mom. I am happy you feel better."

The first thing I noticed was she was not having her coffee as she had done every day for her whole life. I asked her if she wanted a cup of coffee and I would be happy to make it for her. She told me it just didn't sound good right now. I let it go thinking it was just a day she was feeling off from her usual self and that she was excited for her sister flying in tomorrow. To look at her, one would not know how gravely ill she was becoming. She didn't know and neither did I.

The signs were beginning. They were ever so slowly, but the biggest one was she was not eating or drinking like normal. She was beginning to lose interest in food and drink that she normally would, like her coffee. She was sleeping so much more and this had continued since coming home from the hospital. As this began occurring, because it was so subtle, I didn't know what this meant at the time. As each day past, it seemed to bring with it, more sleep for my Mom. This meant less time shared together and time was all we had now. I knew that. I am not sure if my Mom knew it then? I had to accept what was happening and changing on a daily basis.

When she was awake, seeing her big smile would bring such comfort to me. To see her smiling, did wonders for my heart and my soul. I loved every moment I spent with her. Listening to anything she wanted to share with me. Her childhood memories, her past loves, her first jobs, Lincoln High School in the 1950's. Her family. Her grandchildren. Her great grandchildren.

For my Mom a good cup of coffee or Hershey's chocolate was like life blood, she loved these! I started to see a pattern beginning to emerge during this week and especially today that my Mom's eating had rapidly declined. I brought her a giant Hershey bar to cheer her up. What woman doesn't love chocolate? I told her it would be on her bed stand in case she had a chocolate urge in the middle of the night. She laughed at me and I laughed too.

We were supposed to complete with the witnesses and a Notary Public for executing her Will, so there were no issues once the time happened. No part of this is easy, but someone needs to be strong for your sick loved one. For my Mom, it was me, her baby daughter that had to have the emotional strength and courage to complete these tasks for my Mama. Wednesday night my Mom seemed to be having a harder day. She slept the most I have seen her sleep since coming home from the hospital. With Auntie M arriving tomorrow morning, I said to my Mom, we would post pone getting her documents executed and take care of it next week, no worries. We have time. She was fine with that.

Mom stayed up on the sofa for about thirty minutes to visit with me. It was nice just to be together. We didn't need to speak a word to each other, we were just together, and that was perfect. Then Mom announced she was tired and wanted her night medicines to sleep. I said okay I will meet you in your room with a drink and your meds. I went and got some water and her pill holders to get her night medicines.

She was putting on the oxygen and laying on her bed. She said,

"I am so excited my sister will be here tomorrow! I can't wait to see her."

I replied, "Mom are you going to get sick from the excitement, like when I was a little girl being excited to go to Disneyland?"

She laughed and said, "Yes."

With a big smile. She had to purposely *not* tell me, when I was a little girl that we were going to Disneyland. I would literally get sick from the anticipation and excitement of going.

I started handing her the medicines and was telling her what each pill was. I noticed she started to have a bit more difficulty trying to swallow even one pill at a time. She said to me, "Ronda, I don't want to take all of those medicines anymore". I had to use my best Poker Face instantly, and without looking freaked out that just three days before she was adamant to want to continue the Plavix and the Lipitor and all of her vitamins, which were all big pills. I let her know what Hospice comfort medicines were and she wanted the pain medicine, the sleeping pill, the nausea pill and the anxiety pill. I said, "Okay Mama, I will update your pill trays. No worries". I smiled at her, as my chest was filled with anxiety and I could see red flags being waved in my head, that she no longer wanted her other medicines! This was another sign.

I asked if she wanted to watch her favorite show and she said no. I noticed her cell phone on the bed stand, with missed calls. Her and Marylou would talk every night over the course of their friendship. Since my Mom fell ill, I did notice less and less calls they had with each other. I also knew that some of her lifelong friends had been calling out of love and concern, but she wasn't up to talking to anyone now. I figured it was just a bad week for her.

After I got her settled I went upstairs and hopped in the shower to just clear my head and my heart. I knew I would have to gear up to be able to walk along with her, on her pathway she's now on. The shower did wonders for myself. I called my Auntie M to confirm her flight time and arrival on Alaska Airlines. I told Auntie I was really glad she's coming now and that Mom is really excited to love and laugh with her sissy. We were just about to hang up when I said, "Okay, I will see you at 6:30 tomorrow evening."

"Um honey, my flight leaves at 6:30am from Portland and I land in San Diego at 9:00 a.m.", Auntie replied.

We laughed and said good thing we talked. She said she could rent a car if she needed to, but had only planned to be with us and to take of her sissy. I assured her it won't be a problem with work. I will take an early lunch. We hung up. I was excited to see Auntie too! I love her so much. This visit will lift my Mom's spirits up.

Thursday, April 5th began. This was also my brother Mike's birthday. I got ready for work, went downstairs to get my Mom's tray ready and her medicines. She was sitting up when I knocked on her door. She said, "Come in honey." She was leaning against her pile of pillows and smiling at me. She looked tired today and I asked if she was feeling okay?

I set her tray down that had some crackers, water, a nutrition drink and her medicines. I knew her appetite was dwindling so I didn't offer too much food. She started to speak, "I couldn't sleep last night. I am so excited to see my sister Marti!" She was smiling from ear to ear. "I feel like I am a little girl on Christmas morning waiting to open the presents".

It was wonderful to see her so cheerful and happy. I felt better knowing she was tired from not getting enough sleep because she was excited. I shared with my Mom that Auntie's plane would land about 9:00am this morning not tonight. We had a good laugh together because we both thought she was flying to San Diego in the evening.

I handed the medicines to my Mom and asked her to please tell me if she starts hurting before three hours because the nurse could call in stronger medicines to keep her comfortable. She said she would let me know. Her health aide would be coming in this morning also and she would be clean and beautiful by the time I dropped Auntie at our house. I gave my Mom a big hug and a kiss and left for work.

I let my supervisor know as soon as I arrived the mix up with the flight arrival of my Auntie and asked to be able to leave at 8:45a.m. to go pick her up a drive her to my house. He said, yes no problem. I thanked him. Luckily I had some afternoon training at work and this would be my last class for our new accounting system. I worked until it was time to leave.

I sent a text message to my Auntie that I was on my way to the airport. Auntie's plane was on time and I made it to Lindbergh Field Airport right on time. I pulled into the airport terminal and there was my beautiful, tall, blonde and tan Auntie with her suitcase standing outside by her terminal. I parked at the airport curb, gave her a giant hug and helped to lift her suitcase into the back of the FJ.

I told her how happy and excited Mom is to see her and that she couldn't sleep last night out of excitement. We both giggled about that. Auntie asked how her big sissy is *really* doing. I looked over at her and tears in my eyes shared with her the steady decline that Mom seems to be on, especially in just one weeks' time.

I said that her sleeping has increased and her appetite has almost dropped to nothing. I told her how glad I was to have her come. It's been an emotional rollercoaster. Auntie said that she wants to help give Ron and I a break while she's here. We are going to all be in a battle and she wants to help. She also said that she will come back in about two months and help then too, as the disease progresses. I was so grateful to have her here. Her recent experience of losing so many close people in her life, made me sad that it's now her big sister, my Mom, that's facing the fight of her life.

We arrived to my townhouse in about thirty minutes. I helped get the suitcases unloaded and Auntie went in the house to go give her sissy a big hug. Mom was lying on the sofa, showered and in fresh clothes. She looked as good as she could. They hugged each other so tightly. I showed Auntie her room and told them I would be back after work and that Ron should be home soon.

I went back to my office and made it through my day. I drove home on auto-pilot. The last couple weeks have taken a toll on me. Between my Mom's illness, work and coping with my own illness of Fibromyalgia, and Ron losing his dad, I felt exhausted emotionally and physically. I was glad when I pulled up to my driveway. My daughters were going to stop by later to see their Grandma and say hi to Auntie. This would be a nice visit.

When I walked into the patio Mom was sitting in her favorite chair visiting with her sissy. It was nice to see my Mom happy. I did notice she wasn't drinking her usual coffee; instead she had a bottle of water. Red flags start waving in my head and I thought "This is two days in a row she hasn't wanted coffee. I know she's not feeling good." This was my warning sign for my Mom. No coffee equals she's feeling ill.

Auntie made a lovely dinner for everyone and we sat out in the patio. Mom ate a few bites of food. I was trying to not to be obvious but I was paying attention. We all visited and shared family stories. It was a nice short evening. I could see that Mom wasn't feeling good and she seemed to be having a harder time breathing. I asked her if she wanted to go inside and I could bring her oxygen machine to the living room. She opted to go rest in her room.

I got her settled and gave her the night medicines. I asked how her pain was and she said she was hurting more. She thought maybe because she was so tired from the excitement. I said I was going to call Hospice and ask a nurse to call. I wanted to make sure she was comfortable and not in pain. I went into the kitchen and placed a call into Hospice. I received a phone call back right away.

I explained the pain level my Mom was in and the perocets were not taking the pain away for long periods. Her nurse asked if she would take the liquid morphine and I said how nervous she was about taking it. Her nurse reminded me that if she could try a few drops under her tongue, she would have instant relief and it wouldn't make her out of it. I walked into my Mom's room and repeated what her nurse suggested. Mom was in a lot of pain and decided she would try the Morphine drops. I hung up with her nurse and got the morphine out. I measured a few drops and applied them under my Mom's tongue.

You could see relief starting to set in. I assured her that this would help in between the pain pills. She said thank you and she was nervous about using the morphine, but she could feel the relief. She was okay with taking it finally. Auntie came in her room to sit with her sister so I kissed Mom good night and I said I would see her in the morning.

I walked into the living room, slumped on the sofa, and my quite tears fell. The thought of losing my Mom was unbearable, however, the fear of the pain she was going to continue having as the cancer overtook her body was the scariest thing I have had to face in my life. I lay on the sofa crying. Tears running down my face like a turned on water faucet.

Auntie came out in the living room and she came over and hugged me. I hugged her back so tightly. She said to me, "Oh honey. I thought I was coming to have a visit with my big sissy, but she is so much sicker than any of us knew." I told my Auntie how sorry I was. Not that I could have done anything different, I was sorry that Auntie had to go through this with her sissy.

Had I known, I would have done more. This was so hard for me to understand. I kept replaying in my mind the events of the last six months. She went to the doctors every month and for blood tests often. She took all of her medicines and ate healthy. Mom seemed to accept this more than any of my family could. In her famous words after she found out, "It is what it is."

That evening as Mom slept, my Auntie and I visited and talked about so many things. She shared about losing her best friend to lung cancer too. She told me that we would not go through this alone and she would be back to help again, when it got worse for my Mom. Having never gone through something like this, I had nothing to cling on to. No knowledge of what was about to happen. The unknown was a scary concept.

My husband came home from his second job and I excused myself from utter physical and emotional exhaustion. I gave Auntie a hug and kiss good night and Ron and I went upstairs. I crawled into bed and pulled the covers up to my chin. I wanted to just pull them over my head. Ron lay down next to me and held me. He asked how Mom was doing and I gave him an update. I let him know she hasn't drank coffee for a couple days now and that worries me. She is barely eating anything either.

I don't remember falling asleep, but I had. I woke up to my alarm going off at 5:00a.m. and hit snooze once. I was just so tired. The alarm went off again and this time I got up, showered and dressed for work. I went in the bathroom and applied makeup to my swollen eye lids, from crying so much last night. When I was done I went downstairs to get a cup of coffee and started assembling Mom's tray with a piece of toast, applesauce, water and pain pills.

I walked down the hall to her bedroom door. I gently knocked and opened the door, walking towards her bed. She woke up when I entered the bedroom. I said

"Good Morning Mama. How are you today?"

She replied, "I'm okay sweetie."

I asked her what her pain level was and she said it was a seven. I offered her the morning pain medicine and some water. I asked her how the liquid morphine worked for her and she said it actually was good. Inside I was jumping up and down. Thankful that she is finally allowing pain relief. I asked her if she would like to have a few drops of it now, as it helps so quickly and she did not protest and said yes. I got the medicine dropper and filled up just a few drops of the morphine and gently applied it under her tongue. I gave her more water to wash it down. I asked her if she wanted a cup of coffee, hoping and wishing she would, but she said no thank you.

I was just about to give her a hug and kiss before I left for work. Then my inner voice spoke to me. We all have that voice that has helped us throughout our lives that told us to turn left instead of turning right, and it saved us from an accident. Growing up all of us had this voice. Some would listen and some wouldn't. I refer to that voice as my inner Angel now. Truly because I did listen to that voice throughout my lifetime and has saved me from peril. I don't mean to sound crazy at all, just truthful and thankful I listened.

So on this Friday morning at 6:00a.m., as I look down at my sweet mama lying in her bed, I literally was in a motion to lean down and hug and kiss her goodbye, when my *inner Angel* said to me, *"You have to stay home today!"* Out of duty to my office, I almost had decided to not listen to this voice. Again it said, *"You have to stay home with your Mom today!"* It wasn't because she looked worse today, but it was the voice and the feeling I had all of a sudden about my Mom.

I said to her, "You know what Mama? I am going to get back into my pajamas and just crawl in bed with you today if that is okay?" She smiled and laughed at me, and said "Sure sweetie. Hop in bed!" So I called into my supervisor to let him know I needed to be home to take care of my Mom today. It was the best decision I had to make all week and worth every single minute!

      I went upstairs and told my husband Ron I was staying home with Mom today and that I had such a strange feeling and my inner voice said to stay home. He understood me and gave me a big hug and kiss before he left for work. He brought me such comfort with his kind words and his love. This helped me and helped my Mom too.

      I went back into her room and lay down with her for a bit and we talked. She said she is happy that Ron is in my life and he is my real angel. I smiled and agreed with her. Mom and I both told each other how much we loved each other. I said to her, "I have been so blessed to have shared all these years with you. I am so glad you moved in with our family. You have been a good Mom and a great grandma and Oma."

      Mom replied to me," Honey I *have* lived a good life. I am blessed with my big wonderful family. My children, my grandchildren and my great grandchildren. I have a wonderful sister and brother and good friends. I am happy with the life I have had and shared." As she said this to me, I was fighting back the tears. Looking at her today, I could *feel* something was different with her, I just didn't know what? I asked if she wanted a cup of coffee and she said no thank you. I think I want to sleep now. I hugged her and said I will be out in the living room. She stayed in bed all morning sleeping.

      Her nurse Marie called on my cell phone and she asked how my Mom was doing. I gave her updates of the continual decline and her increased pain. I let her know she used the liquid morphine last night and this morning she took more of a dose. Marie was going to consult with her oncologist and get morphine pills called in. She let me know she would come in this afternoon for a check on my Mom.

      She asked me if there were any services she could help us get and I asked her if she could get a chaplain to come over today to offer some prayers for her. Marie said she would send in the referral and the chaplain would contact us. I thanked her and said we would see her later.

Auntie M and I sat in the living room talking. She started going through the Hospice folder that was given to Mom and I and she took out a pamphlet. She asked me if I had read it yet? I said no I hadn't. She began to read it and I went outside to sit in the patio to reflect on everything. I just couldn't believe that my Mom was *dying* from cancer. This was so emotionally difficult to cope with.

My cell phone rang and the number showed "Hospice" as the caller, so I answered right away.

"Hello this is Ronda," I said. There was a woman on the other end,

"Hello Ronda. My name is Marie and I am a chaplain with Hospice. Your Mom's nurse said that you would like a chaplain to come to your home for your Mom?"

"Yes please," I said. "My Mom seems like she's slipping more and more as each day passes and I thought she would be comforted with some prayers."

My family and I commented that it was another *M* name for Mom. This was a small comforting coincidence. The chaplain said she could come out about 11:00 if that would be okay and I said yes.

I walked back into the living room and Auntie was wiping some tears away, when she said to me, "Ronda, you and the family all need to read this pamphlet. It will help you understand what your mama is going through." I took the pamphlet, sat down on the sofa and began to read it. The pamphlet was wrote to help families deal with what their loved one will go through. It was maybe ten pages.

As I read through each page my heart began to race with overwhelming anxiety and tears began rolling down my cheeks. According to this little pamphlet, my Mom was closer to leaving than she was to living much longer. Of course that's not what was wrote, but it described what happens months before death and a generalized course of what will happen.

What made my heart race and the tears start was the things that she has been doing, such as her appetite is gone. She sleeps more than she is awake. She has a loss of interest in things she once enjoyed. She had already been doing this for a few weeks. I hugged my Auntie and she hugged me back. "Auntie, she sicker than we all knew! This isn't fair, it's just not fair!" I excused myself and went upstairs to my bedroom.

I called my brother and my sisters to let them know of our Mom's decline. So if they could make it out to San Diego they should try to come out soon. I let them know I asked for a chaplain to come out for Mom and give her some comforting prayers and that her nurse was coming out today again to check on her. I let them know her appetite is gone and she is in more pain. They are going to probably start morphine pills to help and once they don't relieve her pain then she will go on the morphine pump. I told them I was sorry and I love them.

I came downstairs and it was just about 11:00 when my cell phone rang and it was "Hospice". "Hello, this is Ronda." It was Marie the chaplain and she asked where she could park. I directed her to my neighbor's carport next to mine, as she was so kind to allow Hospice to park there during the day when she was at work. I went outside to greet her and thanked her for coming out. We walked into my home and she introduced herself to my Auntie M.

I let her know about my Mom and her faith. I let her know of my Mom's current state and that we thought prayers would bring her some comfort. Marie asked if she could go on in alone with her, and my Auntie and I both said yes of course. I directed her to Mom's room and Marie walked into my Mom's room. She was in there for a good twenty to thirty minutes when she came out and joined us in the living room.

Marie told us that she asked my Mom many questions and they prayed together. She told us that given her current physical state she would not be surprised if her nurse will say that my Mom is eminent. Auntie M asked what that meant? How long does that mean. Marie replied, "Eminent could mean a matter of days. When we talked she told me that she didn't have any regrets. She didn't feel like she had unfinished business left to do. She said that she has had a wonderful life full of love from her family and that she's ready to go home with her Mom and Dad." Marie then offered us a prayer and Auntie M and I prayed with her for my Mom and for my family. We thanked her for her time and she left.

My Auntie and I stood there stunned to hear what we were already fearing and that was that my Mom was in her last days. Thank goodness, my husband Ron came home from work. I walked up to him and hugged him tightly. I shared with him Mom's decline and that what the chaplain had just told us that my Mom said. It felt like the room was spinning around and I couldn't stop it. We were supposed to have months together not days!

I handed Ron the pamphlet that Auntie had me read. I explained that it's important and will help him to understand where my Mom is in her illness. He opened and read each page until he too started to cry softly. There was no way to sugarcoat the graveness of my Mom's illness and the progression she is at. I didn't know how to tell my children that Grandma is so very sick. They would all stop in tonight and I would share the pamphlet.

Today was Good Friday and Easter was approaching. Our family had decided to celebrate on Saturday together so everyone could be together. We had planned an Easter egg hunt for my grandchildren and we had planned to push Oma in the wheelchair out by the grass, so she could be part of it too. Auntie M and I planned to go get groceries once the nurse stopped in.

It was about 1:00pm when Mom got out of bed for the first time all day. She walked out into the dining room and sat at the table. I asked her if she wanted to eat anything or a drink of something? She said just some water would be good. She said how nice the chaplain was and that they a nice visit. As I sat there with Mom, I looked on the table on the new camcorder was sitting there.

Last weekend Ron and I picked it up so I could record Mom, but we hadn't used it yet. I picked it up and turned it on. I panned to my Mom and pushed record. I began by saying

"Hi Mama. It's almost Easter."

She said, "Happy Springtime! It's a beautiful day."

She smiled. I asked her what her earliest memory was of Easter and she shared a story I had never heard before. Her parents had been in Mexico and brought her and her sister big sombrero hats for their Easter baskets. Once she was done sharing her story, I said okay we will talk again soon and she waived bye, blew a kiss and smiled so big.

She asked for her pain medicines and I gave her some. She went to lay back down and get the oxygen back on. Her nurse arrived shortly after she went into her room. I updated her nurse with her current state and said that she is in a constant decline. My Auntie M told the nurse what the chaplain had said about her condition being eminent. Her nurse went into my Mom's room to check her vitals and talk to her.

The nurse came out about ten minutes later and said that she agreed that my Mom was declining just since yesterday. She also said she had got authorization for the morphine pills. These were a stronger dose and would help with her increased pain.

She said she would still be able to communicate while on the pills and that she had shared this with my Mom. The nurse said she would come by tomorrow to check on her too. I thanked her and she left.

Auntie and I drove to the store to get the Easter groceries. We picked up the items we needed and Auntie got all the kids' baskets with goodies in them. Auntie and I were loading up the groceries in my FJ when I got this horrible foot cramp from wearing "exercise" sandals. It hurt but we were both laughing. Maybe from the stress and the stupid exercise sandals helped me to get this foot cramp, but it wouldn't go away. Auntie had to drive us back to my house. We laughed and laughed about it. As soon as we pulled up to my home, I threw the sandals in the trash and shared with Ron what happened. It was nice to have a few laughs because lately there had been so many tears.

Ron and my son Michael brought the groceries in the house and all helped to unpack them. Auntie asked if Mom had been up at all, and they said no. Auntie was making dinner that night which was a lovely spinach salad with strawberries and a barbeque. Ron helped with the barbeque.

We were all just about to sit down when Mom got up. It was such a pleasant surprise to see her up. She sat down at her favorite seat at the patio table. I watched her use the salad tongs and she picked up one strawberry, one spinach leaf and one small bite of meat. I asked her if she wanted coffee and she said no, water was fine. We visited and shared the funny story of my foot cramp after grocery shopping. We all laughed about it.

During this dinner, I tried to not look obvious of watching my Mom, but I could see her just pushing around the little bit of food on her plate. She had not taken a bite of anything. She just pushed the food around, as she shared in the conversations. Finally she took one small bite of meat and a small bite of the strawberry. Ron took our plates being the gentleman that he is.

I could see my Mom was having difficulty breathing and asked if she wanted to go inside for the oxygen machine? She said yes that sounded like a good idea. I brought out the oxygen machine to the living room and got Mom settled on the couch. You could see the relief in her breathing, once back on the oxygen. The pharmacy knocked out our door and her morphine was here. I signed for it and gave her the dosage. I reminded her that this will help to take the pain away and she could still be awake.

Ron left for work to his second job. Michael went to play video games in his room and Brittney came by for a short visit. Addie had texted that she had to work but would be here tomorrow with Brendon. It was a nice visit. I had walked in the kitchen and Brittney followed me. She couldn't believe how bad Grandma was doing just since a couple days ago. I agreed and told her that we will have to make the best of every minute we have with her. I gave her a hug. I offered Britt the pamphlet to read. I told her that it really describes where Grandma is at. She started to cry after reading it too. The reality of the end of the illness was there. Brittney wiped her tears and then went back into the living room.

Brittney went and hugged Grandma and said she would see her tomorrow for Easter Dinner and the egg hunt with Jake and Josh. Auntie M, my Mom and I were in the living room and it was around the time for the ghost shows. I asked Mom if she wanted to watch it? She said oh yes that would be good. I turned it on. About five minutes into the show, Mom got up very quickly and went into the bathroom. Auntie got up to go see if she needed help.

Mom said she needed to lay down. Auntie help her sister into her bed and I brought the oxygen machine back to Mom's room. Mom was almost getting physically sick. I got the anti-nausea medicine from the Hospice comfort medicines. Auntie helped her take it. We got the oxygen back on my Mom and then her body was calming down and her breathing was getting back in rhythm.

I told Auntie I wanted to talk to my Mom for a moment please. She understood and walked out so we could talk. I sat on the bed next to my Mom and held her hand. I looked into her beautiful brown eyes and said, "Mama. This is so hard for me to say, but I need to say it for you. It's okay if you don't want to eat anymore. It's part of it. It's okay if you don't want to drink anything. These are normal things we do for our bodies, but your body is sick and it's okay if you can't do these things anymore. I love you with all my heart and you have been a good Mom to me and to Diana, Mike and Crystal. You have been such a good Grandma, Oma and Sister. I don't want you to suffer. I don't want you to feel like you *have* to stay here because of any of us. None of us want you to suffer. It's okay if you have to go Home. We will all be okay. We will miss you so much but we will know you are not in pain anymore."

My Mom continued holding my hand and said, "Honey I love you. You have been a good daughter to me. We have been blessed to have all this time. I love my kids, my grandkids and great grandkids and my brother and sister. I have had a good life Ronda. I'm glad you have Ron now, he is really your angel and I know you will be okay." With such a heavy heart I gave my Mom a hug and kiss goodnight and walked into the living room. Auntie went into her sisters' room to talk to her too.

I turned the TV off and opened a bottle of wine. When Auntie came back out we drank wine together. I shared with Auntie what I said and she looked at me and said she told her it's okay to go too. We both just couldn't believe the progression of Mom's *rapid* decline. We talked about so many things that evening and finished a bottle of wine. By the time Ron came home from work I was a bit tipsy.

I updated my husband with what had transpired that evening with Mom and how sick she became. Auntie M had said that her liver couldn't tolerate food anymore because of the cancer. No matter how much I knew my Mom's cancer was taking its toll and her now frail body, it was difficult to handle. I thought I would have had fifteen more years with her before her cancer. Then after finding out she had terminal cancer, we were told four-six months, but even that timeline didn't ring true for my Mom. I felt it had been shortened even from that.

Before my husband and I became an item I let him know that I was a package deal. At that time two of my three teens lived at home, my youngest grandson and of course my Mom lived with me. I let my husband know and understand that my Mom would always live with me no matter what. He said he understood and that wouldn't be a problem.

I said good night to Auntie M and said I would see her in the morning. I walked upstairs and sat down at my computer to search symptoms of terminal stage 4 lung cancer and found information that rang so true with what my Mom was experiencing. I had not searched or researched for this information before this night. I like to be well informed on any subject so that I can appropriately handle a situation, and now I need to know about this.

Terminal Stage Four Lung Cancer is not anything I had ever needed to learn about before in my life. Those words existed. This type of cancer existed. I had no need to read about this until now. Even when my Mom was diagnosed, I stayed clear of the internet on symptoms of Lung Cancer. In this great age of technology and the internet, information is literally a click away on any subject. Knowing that, I think I had feared or dreaded what I would read.

So I logged onto to the internet that Friday night. Typed in *those* words and pressed enter. Pages and pages appeared on this subject. I looked at who the website was from before I clicked a link. There a few medical sites I trust, so I went to those and began reading what the symptoms of terminal stage 4 lung cancer were. Extreme fatigue, increased sleeping, coughing, wheezing, shortness of breath, loss of weight, loss of appetite, increased pain and nail and skin discolorations.

What I found was consistent with my Mom's symptoms. Her loss of appetite, her breathing becoming difficult, her pain and her increased sleeping, but the one that freaked me out the most was the purple blotchy skin on her hands and arms! This was definitely and end sign of one suffering from lung cancer created by lack of oxygenated circulatory blood flow. I can vividly remember asking her regular doctor about these purple marks on her hands and arms and we were told it was just that her skin was thin and from her medicines. I sat and cried as I read this knowing that my Mom had these signs for at least a couple months already.

It was like snap shots going through my head, of the last few months with my Mom's health. As I thought about my Mom and what lead us to urgent care on March 15th, it was becoming clear that Mom was ill months before we went to urgent care. Her purple skin spots I had asked about during the doctor visit in December. Her fatigue had been increasing on a slow downward spiral of inactivity. All the recent outings she turned down with me or with Marylou up to her illness. The final snap shot was when I realized all the fresh food we had bought for my Mom and son, before my husband and I went to New York for Ron's dad's funeral, all that food was seemingly untouched. It was not that my Mom and Michael went to dinners; it was because my Mom lay in pain and her desire to not eat had already begun.

I closed my lap top and I lay in my husband's comforting arms. Crying so deeply and sorrowfully. My husband in his sweet kindness tried to comfort me. At that moment, there was not a word anyone could have said to me to make me feel better or to stop the tears from falling like rain. My Mom was dying and there was nothing I could do for her but continue to love her and keep her out of pain.

CHAPTER 6 - THE SPIRITUAL JOURNEY

The spiritual journey can happen within a few weeks, days or hours before the final physical goodbye. This part can only be travelled by your ill loved one. It may start out so subtlety at first and will grow intensely near the end. Where there is a gentle pulling away from life, activities, and people and even friends and family. Everyone's spiritual journey is their own and no two experiences will be the same. During this time where your loved one is sleeping far more than they are awake, in their unconscious mind, in their dreams, they are free from cancer, free to remember and reflect on their life. They are becoming closer to stepping to the other side than they are closer to this physical side.

Spirituality in itself has its own unique belief of the individual. We are raised through our own family's beliefs to then share with our families. This is something shared across the world and in so many different ways and religions. I was lucky that my Mom allowed me to experience every religion that I wanted to learn about. She never told me we were one religion or another, or that this religion is the correct one compared to any others. I went with all of my friends to all of their churches as a young girl. In our home we were Christian and I had a step-dad who was Jewish, so we had celebrated all the holidays. Having had such a broad base of spirituality has provided my beliefs that I have today.

Mom was very spiritual and had a strong belief that there is more to this life and that we are blessed with Angels. I can remember before my Nana passed, my Mom's mother. I didn't know it then, on the last day when I was at the hospital visiting Nana, that would be my last moments with her physical self. I do remember sensing my Papa's presence, her husband. I vividly remember the calm expression on my Nana's beautiful face. She couldn't speak and she never woke up, and she was at peace. Looking back to that day, my Nana was on her spiritual journey.

    Mom was living in Iowa at the time Nana was in the hospital, and she later shared a wonderful spiritual story with me. The day she was leaving to the airport to fly back to San Diego to come see her Mom. Mom was given Nana and Papa's 50th wedding anniversary clock. It was the kind in the glass dome that you could see the golden clock mechanisms inside and the clock used to chime. On this day, that anniversary clock started to chime again after years of not. My Mom felt it was a sign from Papa, her dad that he was coming back for his beloved "Honeychild". Was it pure coincidence that their anniversary began to chime on this same day, Nana passed? I like to think it was a spiritual sign.

    Saturday morning April 7th, I woke up early and immediately went downstairs to check on my Mom. I knocked on her door and I opened it slowly. She was just waking and I had to put on the best poker face of my life. When I walked over to my Mom, she was entirely different from just last evening at bedtime. She had a different look on her face, more distant and less coherent. I could *feel* the presence of Nana and Papa in her room, as strange as that may sound, and I half disregarded those feelings or sensations, because I knew her time was soon.

    I asked her how her pain was and she said she needs her pain medicine. I got her morphine pills and anti-nausea medicine for her. She had a bit of difficulty swallowing this morning. I sat on the edge of the bed just to be with her. I held her hand. As the sound of the oxygen machine puffed with each of her labored breaths, I told her how much I loved her. I reminded her that we were going to celebrate Easter today with all the kids and my grandchildren today. I said that when it was time for the Easter Egg hunt, I could push the wheelchair under the shady trees on the grass and hide eggs around her for the kids. We both laughed about that. I said to her, that we would do that only if she was up to it of course. I asked if she wanted coffee or anything. She said no thank you.

    I reminded her that her brother, my Uncle John, would be here on Tuesday and he was looking forward to seeing her. She smiled and said "Me too." I updated her that my brother Michael was trying to leave tomorrow from Spokane, so he should be here soon too. She nodded and just seemed so sleepy and distant. I said I was going to go start cooking but I would check on her and if she wanted to come out to the sofa I would bring the oxygen machine for her. Auntie M had just walked in her bedroom and I excused myself after I gave Mama a kiss. My Auntie and I didn't even need to say a word to each other, as we both knew what was happening.

    I went in the kitchen to make some coffee and to wake up some more. I was lost in my thoughts of my Mom. Auntie M joined me shortly and we both hugged tightly. We both knew and didn't have to say anything. My Mom's spiritual journey was well under way. Over-night, in her sleep, it was as if her soul began packing for her next journey from this life for her spiritual journey she was now on.

    I called the Hospice number to ask to speak to her nurse, they said they would have her call. She called within ten minutes. I let her know the state of my Mom and the disbelief that this day arrived so quickly. Her nurse said she would come stop in about 10:00am and I said that was fine. I hung up and tears started in my eyes and then I couldn't stop. I felt like I had never cried so much in my entire life, as I had in the last few weeks. I called my sisters and left my brother a message. I wanted them to know if they could come, they need to try now.

    I made myself busy by chopping and getting food ready for an early dinner with the family. I was lost in my own silent thoughts and reflections with my Mom. All the holidays we shared, the good times, the sad times, the laughter and the love, this was it. We have shared all our final ones together. I prayed for strength, I prayed for my Mom not to suffer or be scared. I prayed for my kids, my grandkids, for my brother, my sisters, my Auntie M and Uncle J. We were the ones that would need our strength to hold each other up.

When most of the food was prepped or cooking, I went into Mom's room to check on her. She was in such a deep, deep sleep. The only sound was of the oxygen puffing with her breath. She didn't wake with my presence like she always had before. I just looked at her sleeping and thought, "Oh Mama. I love you so much. I can't imagine my life without you in it. I'm so sorry you are sick." I couldn't get over the feeling in her room. There was definitely a presence of love in her room, like if angels were present.

I walked out to the patio and sat down in her chair. I looked to the rolling, rocky hillside across the street that she loved looking at. I looked at the view that she enjoyed in her last few weeks. All the trees around, birds chirping and I could see why she liked the Springtime. I looked around the patio that she enjoyed. She called our patio the secret garden. I sat there in her chair for comfort, as she was on her spiritual journey. I could only love her and keep her body comfortable now, and keep her out of pain.

Her nurse opened our back gate and I welcomed her in. She gave me a hug and walked in the house. She said she was going to check on Mom and do her vitals. Auntie and I sat on the sofa and talked while her nurse was back there. She came out after a few minutes and said she was surprised to see the decline of her since yesterday. She ordered Mom a personal bathroom chair for her bedroom, due to Mom's weakened state.

She explained the use of her morphine pills and using the liquid if she couldn't swallow pills anymore. She said when Mom begins to not swallow she will need the morphine pump that will regulate her medicine dosages and that we could give her an extra small dose if she had breakthrough pain. As we stood there in my living room, her nurse said to my Auntie and I, "I want to let you know there are angels here for your Mom." Auntie and I looked at each other and we said "We know". Her nurse shared that she doesn't usually say something like this to her patients' families, but she felt it as soon as she walked in my Mom's room. We told her we feel them too.

After the nurse left, Auntie said she would like to go to Lowe's to get some flowers to plant in my hanging baskets in the patio. I knocked on Michael's door to let him know we're going to the store and should be back in less than an hour. I let him know Grandma should stay sleeping, so not to worry. Auntie, Ron and I drove to the store, Auntie picked out beautiful colorful flowers and then we drove home.

When we walked in the house, we had such a surprise waiting for us. Mom was up, sitting in the leather chair that is between the living room area and dining room. She was sitting legs crossed and sipping on a chocolate nutrition drink with a straw in it. I said,

"Well hi Mom! Good to see you up."

She smiled and said "It's good to be up! I'm enjoying the beautiful day".

This would be her burst of energy. Auntie M, Ron and I were freaking out inside of our own heads. We all had read about the burst of energy.

We learned that in days before dying from an illness the terminally ill person may have a burst of energy. Not like getting up and spring cleaning, but they will get up and seem like their own self again when they have been so out of it. They may request a meal or a favorite food when they haven't eaten food in weeks, they will be up out of bed, when they have been bedridden and sleeping so much. They might have conversations with family and friends, when they have been more withdrawn.

It almost gives all the caregivers a false sense of hope that their loved one may be okay for a while longer.

I knocked on Michael's door and asked him to come to the living room. I stopped him at his doorway and I quietly whispered ,

"Sweetie, how long was Grandma up?"

He said, "What do you mean up? I thought she was sleeping the whole time."

I told him, " We walked in the house and she was sitting in the leather chair sipping a drink with a straw."

He apologized because he didn't know. I let him know it was okay, we were just not expecting her to be awake. I hugged him tightly, told him it was okay and we joined everyone in the living room.

We visited with her for about fifteen minutes and we enjoyed every single minute. On this day she called my cell phone and left me a message. She said "Hi sweetie. It's Mom. It's a beautiful day and I was calling to say I love you." I cannot even begin to tell anyone how unbelievable and precious that message from my Mom means. To hear her voice is priceless, and as brief as our visit with her was, she soon said, "Well, I'm going to lay down again and rest". I helped her in her room and with the oxygen. I told her to have a nice nap before all the grandchildren arrived. I blew her a kiss and closed her door except for a crack, in case she needed anything.

Her personal bathroom chair arrived and Auntie tied a pretty flower Mylar balloon on the handle for the Princess throne. We put it in her room and Mom woke up and laughed about the balloon. I let her know it would be about two more hours until everyone would arrive. I went and showered and got dressed up. I came downstairs and set the table for a buffet and finished with the last of Easter dinner preparations.

Soon my daughters and their families arrived. The kids were all so excited for their Easter goodies and the Easter egg hunt. They wanted to see their Oma too. I explained to them that Oma is not feeling very good so we need to use our quiet voices and be gentle with her. I opened her door and said "Look who I found Oma!"

She smiled so big and each of her three little great-grandchildren climbed up on her bed. Each little boy took turns to give Oma a hug and kiss and wished her Happy Easter. They stayed sitting on the bed with her. As this was happening I tried videotaping this on the little camcorder we picked up. My daughters all gave their Grandma a hug and kiss. I asked *Oma* if she wanted to go outside to watch the Easter Egg hunt and she said, "Oh sweeties, Oma is just too tired right now, but you go and have fun." The three little boys just stayed sitting on their Oma's bed next to her, until they all were vying for the spot closest to Oma.

I suggested that we let Oma rest right now and asked them to gently get off the bed for the egg hunt. Jake, Josh & Brendon all said "Bye Oma. I love you!" She smiled and said "I love you too." She blew them kisses. I gave the bags of candy and money filled eggs to my three kids to go hide the eggs in the grass area by my townhouse. I asked Mom if she wanted to go outside, I could wheel her out and it's no problem. She said, "No honey. I'm just tired, but you go enjoy." I let her know that was perfectly fine. I asked if she would like to have some Easter dinner when it was ready, even though I knew she wouldn't eat and I had to ask. She said no thanks.

I told her I would see her in a bit. I joined my family outside with my camera. We gave the boys their Easter baskets and started the count down, one, two, three and off their little legs ran around the grass, squealing in delight of the colored eggs filled with treats and money. Big smiles on their faces, pure joy. I smiled outwardly to them, but I was silently thinking about my very ill Mom laying in her room. By late afternoon, that burst of clear and coherent speech she had, like when she sat in the leather chair earlier, was nowhere to be found now. Instead, it was replaced with a weakened, frail, distant woman again, like this morning. She drifted back into her sleep, drifted into her spiritual solitude. She was making her peace of this life.

We received a phone call from Uncle J. He said that he has decided he is leaving Northern California now and driving straight through. He decided to move his dates up to visit his sister. He said he was going to crash at his friend's house in Vista and then would be at our house first thing in the morning. I said okay, please drive safely and that I loved him. I asked Auntie if she knew why the change of plans? She said she didn't know.

As the kids were finishing up outside looking at their egg prizes I was in the kitchen getting dinner set. I called in my daughters to make the kids plates and encouraged everyone to please eat. I went into Mom's room and sat on her bed. She sort of woke up. The sound of the oxygen machine, puffing in and out. I told her that her brother John David decided he couldn't wait any longer and wanted to come see his big sissy, so he is on the road now. She smiled and nodded her head up and down in a motion of yes. I let her know dinner was ready and I wanted to find out if she would like to move into the living room with her oxygen machine? She shook her head no.

I smiled at her and gently lay my hand on hers and said that is fine and it's okay, we all understand. She said it was nice to see the boys and her granddaughters. I agreed that it was nice. I said to her , "You are an amazing woman, Mom, Grandma, Oma. Think of this huge family you created because of your kids. That is priceless. I love you Mama. And it's okay. You will be okay and we will be okay. I need you to know that you have been the best Mom to me and thank you for everything you have done to help our family and for these past years of living together, we will always have those special memories."

She smiled and listened to me. It seemed that processing thoughts and even speaking was hard for her now. I could see it, I could feel it. I gave her a kiss and said I would be in a little bit with her medicines. She just nodded her head for yes. I walked out and joined my family who were under way in eating. I made a very small plate, as I had no appetite, but had to eat because of my diabetes.

I sat and listened to the excitement of the house. My daughters were having a very hard time seeing their Grandma like this. We all were. I had called them earlier to prepare them for her rapid decline. Really how can anyone prepare to see their beloved family member who had been so vital and over flowing with life a month ago, now become so faraway both physically, mentally and spiritually?

After dinner as the kids played, we all sat on the sectional sofa. Addie was sitting between me and Auntie M, and she started crying. After Grandma was diagnosed with terminal cancer she had booked a quick trip to Las Vegas to go get a memorial tattoo for her Grandma. She was really torn about leaving tomorrow. I told her that Grandma would want her to go. Go and do this for herself and for Grandma. She knows how much you love her.

Addie shared with us that she was going to get a hummingbird tattoo for Grandma and we thought that was so sweet, if you are one to like tattoos. As the evening was coming to an end, my daughters went into visit with their Grandma. They each were able to talk with her for a few minutes and tell her what they needed to tell her. My grandsons then went in to tell Oma they loved her. All of our hearts were heavy with the pending loss, except my sweet little grandsons. They had no idea. My heart was breaking for them. We all hugged good-bye and they left.

We opened a bottle of red wine and sat and drank it in the living room. The sound of the oxygen machine had a different sound. Auntie went in first and I followed. Mom was having a harder time breathing. I placed an Ativan under her tongue to help her breathing relax. We were provided information of what to do when her breathing became more difficult. Mom tried to sit up and fell back down on her bed in her weakened state. We asked her what she needed? She said "I need to go to the restroom".

It was at this moment that I now understood why her nurse had ordered the personal chair for her. Mom could not stand up without our help anymore. She could not walk. This was a moment that was difficult for me and I am certain for my Mom. Always a very proud woman, to now be incapable of doing anything for her own self. We helped her use her personal facility chair the Auntie and I got her tucked back into bed. I gave her the liquid morphine dosage. This helped her pain and calmed down her labored breathing.

I called Hospice to talk to a nurse. The nurse returned my call right away. I reported the changes occurring. She was very nice to me. She explained what is happening and that if in my Mom's sleep she starts to gurgle, to use the Atropine drops. She asked if we had received those in her comfort medicines? I said we had. She said we will need to use these to help her. She said she would provide the update for my Mom's nurse. I was a bit shaken up by all this, but I understood what needed to be done.

Auntie came out of her room and said she was going to sleep on the sofa tonight so she could be close to her sister through the night, just in case my Mom needed anything. I let her know what the Hospice nurse had said about the Atropine drops and that we will need to start using them. It was about an hour later that we did need to use this medicine. Just a couple of drops would help dry up the excess salvia.

Auntie suggested that I go get some rest and that she would take care of her sissy tonight. It was after midnight when Ron and I went upstairs. I flopped onto our bed and cried. It was so hard to know that her last days were now, that this was it. My husband hugged me tight and I drifted off to a broken sleep as my Mom continued on her spiritual journey.

CHAPTER 7 - THE FINAL JOURNEY

April 8th, Easter Sunday. I woke up with a jolt. I tried to get my bearings and remembered last night with my Mom. I threw some clothes on and went downstairs to see her. Auntie was asleep on the sofa. I tried to be quiet going down the stairs, but I woke her up. I asked how Mom had done last night. She said "She had a hard night honey."

I walked into my Mom's bedroom first and Auntie followed behind me. All you could hear was the oxygen machine puffing with each of my Mom's labored breaths. I looked at her and she had that very calm and peaceful look that my Nana had on her last day. I whispered, "Oh Mama!" Her eyes opened. Instead of her beautiful brown eyes looking at me, as she had for the past forty-one years of my life, pale covered brown eyes looked towards me.

She seemed to have a puzzled look on her face. I gasped and whispered to Auntie, "She's blind. She can't see!" I touched my Mom's arm and said, "It's me Ronda and your sister Marti is here. It's okay Mama we are here." As tears just rolled down my cheeks, I tried to stay calm and quiet so I didn't upset my Mom. Inside I was screaming, *No. Oh my God, No! This is it. Today is her last day with me!* I could feel an angelic presence and I could feel the presence of my Nana & Papa in her bedroom, so could my Auntie. That may seem strange to some people unless they have ever experienced something like this. I know what I felt and sensed, my Auntie did too. Even in this chaotic moment, there was a beautiful angelic calmness.

I told my Mom that her brother John David is coming over soon. She seemed to nod her head slightly for yes. I told her that her son Mike is on his way from Spokane to come see her too. I wanted to give her some comfort and I just didn't know what else to do or say. One thing I was certain about was this was going to be my Mom's last day. Her whole being was different today. I just couldn't believe just two days ago, she was sitting and talking with me and looked well considering her cancer, to this frail woman. She couldn't speak, she couldn't see.

Our conversations I had come flooding back to me. My Mom said, "*If I had to go in any season, I'm glad it's in Springtime.*" She said that only about a week ago and she must have known. We were supposed to have four to six months, not a week! I told Mom I loved her and I would be back in her room shortly. Auntie remained with her.

I went and called Hospice in hopes to reach her nurse. She was working today, thank goodness. Her nurse called me right back. Through my tears, I told her that Mom is blind, she can't speak and today is her last day. Her nurse said she would be over soon and asked if we needed anything else? I said, "Yes please, we need a Chaplin to come pray for her." She said when we got off of the phone she would put the request in. I thanked her and we hung up.

Uncle John had called Auntie and he would be to our house in about an hour. I called my daughters to tell them of Grandma's change. Addie was just about to fly out of San Diego and she called me back to tell me she was going to have Brendon's other Grandma come and bring Brendon over to give Oma a kiss and hug. I called Brittney and she said would be over soon. I woke up my Michael to tell him about Grandma change. He went into her room and gave her a hug and kiss and he told her that he loved her.

We were all crying. It was such an emotional morning. I was just about to call my sisters and brother when her nurse arrived to our house. She gave us a hug and said she would go in and look in on Mom. Uncle John arrived next and then Brittney. Her nurse came out of the bedroom and recommended that she order the morphine pump to keep her pain free in her day or days she had left. She told me that once the pump is hooked up, that my Mom would not wake up again.

This was a horrible decision to have to make, but I promised my Mom I would not have her suffer and that I would be her voice when she didn't have one. I already knew on this morning when she opened her eyes and she was blind. She tried to speak and couldn't, I knew in my heart, today was the day that I would be her voice. I asked her nurse to please order the pump. She said to call her when it arrives and she will come back to get my Mom hooked up.

My Uncle J went back to see his big sissy and to talk to her. My heart was breaking at the loss we all were about to have to face. The loss of not having her in our lives, was so great. Auntie and I went into her bedroom and my Mom opened her eyes one more time feeling her brother and us in the room. Brittney went in next and my son Michael followed. I knew this was going to be very difficult for them to see their Grandma like this. They were so close to her, just like I was. I wasn't prepared for this day either. It had come too fast, too soon.

I walked back into the living room and was about to call my brother and sisters, when there was a knock on my front door. It was the Hospice Chaplain. I welcomed him into my home, thanked him for coming her for my Mom and on Easter Sunday. He was a very kind, older man. We shared a bit about my Mom, her family and her spiritual beliefs. I told him that I felt this was going to be her last day with us and I wanted to make sure she had some comforting prayers to send her onto her next journey.

The Chaplain asked us all to join him in her bedroom. He then asked us to please surround to please take part in this blessing for Mom. I stood up by her head and my kids, my husband, my Auntie M and my Uncle J filled in around her bed. The Chaplain turned on some beautiful angelic music that played so softly and he began the most beautiful and touching blessing I have ever heard in my life.

During the blessing we laid hands onto my Mom as the Chaplain read this blessing aloud. It was so moving to all of us in the room. When he spoke of her hands that held her babies so tight, I lost it and couldn't stop crying. Mom had raised the four of us and she had participated in her twelve grandchildren and seventeen great-grandchildren's lives. I knew her hands would never cradle another baby, would never hug any of us again. My heart was breaking.

The Chaplain went on with a very traditional prayer from the bible. When he was done and we all said amen. There was a new peace about my Mom. Again, you could sense my grandparents spirits waiting to bring her home and a beautiful angelic presence that we all felt. We walked out in the living room and thanked the Chaplain again. He gave us his card and said to please call anytime.

I finally was able to call my sisters. I walked into the hallway, just outside of my Mom's bedroom. I spoke to my oldest sister Diana first. I let her know our Mom's progression and that I felt this would be her last day. I said to my sister through tears, "Mom can't see anymore and she can't speak, but she can hear. I know how much you were trying to get here for her, but this day came sooner than any of us could have known. I am going to hold the phone to her ear so you can talk to her and please say *anything* and *everything* you need to say to her."

I walked into her room and let Mom know that her daughter Diana was on the phone and she's going to talk to her. I placed the phone next to her hear and announced to Diana that the phone is by her ear. That conversation was private between my Mom and my sister. Our Mom tried to talk, but just unrecognizable sounds came out. After a few minutes I put the phone to my ear and asked if she was done talking to Mom? We cried. I said how sorry I was and told her that I need to reach Mike and Crystal still. I told her I loved her and we hung up.

Next, I tried calling my brother, as he was the next oldest. I couldn't reach him so I left a message to call as soon as he could. I dialed my sister Crystal and I told her what I had said to Diana through tears. I let our Mom know her daughter Crystal was on the phone and was going to talk to her too. Mom could hear her daughter talk, those last words that was only between the two of them. Our Mom tried to communicate, but couldn't speak any words, just sounds. After a few minutes I put the phone back to my ear and asked my sister if she was done saying what she needed to say. She said yes. We cried together and then we hung up.

I walked outside to get some air. This was so difficult. I tried calling my brother again, no answer. I called Marylou, my Mom's best friend to tell her about Mom. I said to her, "I don't know if you want to see her like this? She looks so different." Marylou said that she wanted to remember her best friend as she was. I told her I understood. Then I called our family friend Kashious.

He was going to try to get out the weekend before, but things came up and he couldn't make it. Kashious was my husband's best man at our wedding in the sands on Coronado Island by the Hotel Del. That was such a beautiful day we shared and my mama was there. Kashious is an R & B singer. He has such a beautiful voice. During any family gatherings, if Kashious was there, I would ask him to sing for me and my Mom. Mom loved him so much and loved his singing.

This morning was difficult and what I had to tell him, "Kash. Today is Mom's last day with us. If you want to come and give her a hug and say goodbye, then you should." He was just as surprised to hear those words from my mouth, as I was to say them. He told me he was definitely coming down. We hung up and I cried.

I was so glad we had yesterday together. I let Uncle J and everyone know that there were left overs in the fridge. Please make yourself at home. Through this day, everyone took turns visiting with Mom. Our neighbors brought us tulip flowers, that was very sweet. I got a call from Addie that Brendon was on his way over to see Oma to give her a hug and kiss. Soon, Sandy drove up to our house. This is Brendon's other Grandma. It was very important to Addie that Brendon came to see his Oma one last time.

Mom and Brendon were so close. He's a very bright three year old and I didn't know how he would handle this once Oma was an Angel in Heaven. Brendon knocked on my back gate, "Nana. I'm here," he announced. I went and opened the gate for him to come in. He gave me a big hug and said, "Nana, I came to see Oma. Can I go see her?" I said, "Of course sweetie." We walked into Oma's bedroom. I told him she was very tired and didn't feel good. He climbed on her bed, without reservation, and gave her a big hug and a kiss on her cheek. He said to her, "Oma, I love you. I'm going to go." He climbed off her bed and blew her a kiss goodbye and walked out of her bedroom.

I walked him outside to his Grandma Sandy and thanked her for bringing him by the house. She said she had to for him. Addie had called and told her how sick her Grandma was and asked if she could please bring him by. We hugged and they left. I stood outside for a moment and cried. I thought that would be the last time he will see his beloved Oma and it just broke my heart.

I walked back in the house and Auntie and I went in Mom's bedroom. We stood there hugging each other. Auntie looked over to my Mom's brand new Bellini boot box and said to me, "Oh dammit. Your Mom didn't get to wear her new boots. She told me on Thursday she was upset because she didn't have a chance to wear them yet." We smiled with that statement of my Mom. Miss Fashion Queen. Auntie and I asked each other if we should put her boots on her, so at least my Mom could say she got to wear them? We laughed about it, knowing Mom's since of humor, she would probably have wanted us to do that, but we decided against it.

Ron knocked on the door and said the morphine pump had arrived. I walked into the kitchen and called Hospice. I asked them to please call my Mom's nurse because the morphine pump had arrived. Her nurse called me right back and said she was just finishing up with another patient and would be right over.

Kashious opened the back gate and walked inside the house. We hugged each other and I thanked him for driving down to see Mom. He said that he had too and that he loved her too. I walked into her bedroom with Kash and he looked at her and started to cry. This big tall teddy bear of a man, I had never seen him cry. He said that he had no idea how ill she was. I told him, none of us did. He was sorry for not coming by last weekend and I said you are here now and she knows. I walked out in the living room to give him some time to talk to her.

Her nurse was next to arrive to my home. This day seemed like a constant stream of family and friends. Her nurse Marie picked up the package and Auntie and I went into the bedroom while she was hooking up the pump. She explained that the morphine pump was like a timer releasing the correct dosage to keep my Mom out of pain. She showed us a little push button that we could push if it seemed like she was in pain between doses. She reminded us to continue using the Atropine by dropping in a couple drops into her mouth to help with the extra saliva. She gave us a hug and said to call Hospice if we need anything or have any questions. She also said the Angels are here. We nodded at her in agreement and she left.

As we stood there looking at Mom sleeping. There was not a wrinkle on her face, smooth and peaceful. Her jaw was slightly opened now. We could only hear the sound of the oxygen puffing with each of her labored breaths and the sound in the back of her throat. I had heard the saying of *The Death Rattle* before, and until this day, I didn't know what that meant. This sound can occur days before someone has been ill and is on their final journey of dying.

I was so sad. I felt so helpless. There was nothing more I could do to help my dying Mom. My Auntie looked at me and said, "Honey, you do know that this is now only her body here. Her spirit is not." She was trying to comfort me. At this point I could find no comfort with any words. We joined the rest of the family in the living room and visited for a bit.

I walked back in her room and climbed on her bed. I lay down next to her sleeping body. I reached out and placed my hand on her hands that were on her stomach. I told her how much I loved her and thanked her for all the kindness and love she has given to our family. I told her how much I would miss her, but it was okay for her to go Home. I cried softly as I lay there with my Mom.

I fell asleep without meaning too. This was a very emotionally exhausting day. However, the most amazing gift happened as I took my last nap with my Mom. I was having the most vivid dream of my life! In this dream, I opened my eyes to Mom holding my hand. It was a view as if I were a small girl looking up to her. She was young woman and was strikingly beautiful. She seemed to be in her late twenties with long black hair flowing hair. There was a glowing aura of light all around her, around everything. As she held my hand and we walked together, she was smiling at me. We were in the most beautiful place I had ever seen in my life. It was so full of color, every color. I couldn't tell you the hues of this spectrum except that they all became a white light that enveloped everything.

This place was love. It was life. It was spiritual. It was surreal. My Mom led me through this spiritual place walking on what seemed to be rolling puffy clouds of meadows. She never said a spoken word to me, but I heard her tell me she was going to be alright. I would see her again here. Then, this beautiful place of white light and love became dim quickly. I felt pulled back into the bed, lying next to my Mom's sleeping body. I was awakened by her labored breaths. I looked at her face then as I took my hand off of hers, I could see that her hands were a blueish purple color. I kind of panicked.

I quickly got off her bed and went to find Auntie and Uncle, "Her hands are purple. Her hands are purple!" I said. They went into her bedroom. My husband hugged me and I started to cry. I knew it would be hours now. This physical sign was that there is not enough oxygenated blood flow happening in her body. Creating a purple color to her hands and her feet.

I tried calling my brother again. He had to be able to talk to her one last time. He finally was able to call me back. I updated our Mom's condition and that I would put the phone to her ear. She could hear, but she can't talk. I told my brother to tell her anything he needs too and that I was sorry. I held the phone to her ear and my brother spoke his final words to her. She recognized his voice. She never opened her eyes but she made some sounds as if trying to tell him she loved him. I put the phone back to my ear and asked him if he was done talking to her? He said he was. I told him I love him and we hung up.

Once Mom finally was able to hear all of her children again, there seemed to be a release in her. It was as if she held on all day so her brother could get here and to be able to hear her children's voices one last time. I was so sorry that my brother and sisters couldn't be here and they were too. Two days ago she seemed okay, and yet two days later, she's almost completed her journey of life and beginning the new journey of death.

The sun was down now and the twilight sky began to over-take the light. We were all visiting in the living room and Auntie shared some beautiful moments from today. She told us that earlier when my daughter Brittney went in to see Grandma, she had laid her head on Grandma and was crying so hard.

Grandma opened her eyes and spoke to Brittney. She said, "Honey, I love you so much." This was so wonderful to hear. She hadn't been able to speak all day, yet even as her spirit was transitioning from this world to the next, my Mom's loving kindness came through to comfort her grand-daughter.

Then Auntie shared, something we find moving to all of us. Auntie had been in the bedroom earlier this afternoon, Mom opened her eyes looking at something, but not at my Auntie, and said, "And there you are! That's awesome!" We feel she reunited with her parents in her spiritual home and this brought all of us such comfort.

It was about 7:45pm that evening. The hallway light was on that led to Mom's bedroom. We all were just hanging out together in the living room, when the hallway light all of a sudden got really bright for a moment and then it dimmed very low. The adrenaline rushed through my entire body and I bolted up from the sofa and went running into my Mom's room. I had asked her to flick the lights so I would know she's there after she left this world. This light had *never* done this before that moment.

I went to check on her and she was still breathing, but ever so hard. The sound of the oxygen machine puffed. I clicked her medicine pump, hoping to help her stay out of pain. I told her I loved her. I walked out and told everyone she's still with us and shared the light story with them. My whole body hurt after that. I was so worried that was it and she was saying to me, she's okay. I walked outside from the patio into my carport and sat in the back of my FJ. My husband joined me.

We sat there for only a few minutes and talked about everything. Uncle J came out and gently said to me, "It's time." Hearing those words were what my heart had been dreading. I knew this morning, today, was my Mom's last day. I could feel it. I could see it happening, but I didn't want to accept it. What would I do without her in my life? I'm sure she felt just as robbed of life and time in it, as I did.

I don't remember walking or running into my Mom's bedroom, but I was in her room. The oxygen machine no longer was puffing. My kids and my Auntie we're standing by her bed and I climbed up on her bed as fast as I could get to her side. My heart was racing and my blood pumped through my body. I put my hand on her chest and could feel, thump thump, thump thump. I said,

"She's still with us. I can feel her heart beating!"

My Auntie walked up and picked up my hand and she said to me,

"Oh honey, that's your own pulse beating, she's gone."

I laid my head on my Mom's chest and just sobbed. I know all of the family was in her bedroom, but in that moment, I felt completely alone and the loss I felt was so heavy in my heart. I hugged my Mama as I cried and whispered in her ear that I loved her so much. A lifetime of memories came flooding back up to this single moment. My Mom was gone. She passed away at 8:00p.m. on Easter Sunday, twenty-five days to the hour that Ron & I first brought her to urgent care. I finally climbed off the bed and hugged my Uncle and my Auntie. I hugged my children and then my husband. Everyone gave my Mom their last hug.

I walked into the kitchen and called the Hospice number and through tears told the person that answered, that my Mom, Marybeth had just passed away. The stranger on the other end of the phone gave their condolences and would send out the nurse. I requested to please have a Chaplain come to my house for a final prayer for my Mom. I then called my sister's and could barely get the words out, "I'm sorry but Mom is gone." That was so brutal to have to tell them and I can't imagine how it felt for them to have to go through this loss so far away from our Mom.

I tried calling my brother but only got his cell phone voice mail. I just asked him to call right away.

I couldn't call anyone else. I couldn't talk. I couldn't think. I could barely breath. Trying to deal with the fact my Mom had been diagnosed with Terminal Cancer was hard enough, but she left us so much sooner than even the doctors knew. I let the family know that the Hospice nurse would be coming out and a Chaplain would come to say a prayer for her. My brother called and my husband Ron answered the phone. He tried to hand me the phone and I looked at him and said, "I can't talk right now. I can't tell him." I felt so bad that my husband had to tell my brother. At that moment, I felt like I had been punched in the chest and couldn't breathe. It was like the day at the hospital, when the pulmonologist told me and Brittney, that my Mom had cancer.

I went and sat out in the patio and cried. My husband came and sat with me. He hugged me. He told me that he let my brother know that Mom had passed. I was so thankful to have him here right now. Someone opened some wine and we all had a glass. That helped calm us some. After a while, we opened another bottle. We all laughed and said if the nurse didn't get her soon we all might be drunk by the time she arrives. I love that my family tries to have humor and laughter in times of sorrow. Every family reacts so differently.

Soon the Hospice nurse arrived at our house. She introduced herself and offered her condolences. I walked her into my Mom's room and she said she needs to remove the morphine pump and asked if I could gather her medicines. I had them in a plastic shoe tub and set them on the table by the bed. I said I was going to go in the living room while she did what she needed to do.

I was simply stunned by the events of the last forty-eight hours. It was so hard to believe that just two days ago I was talking and laughing with my Mom. Listening to her favorite

Easter memory about the year her parents gave them Easter Sombreros filled with candy. Had I not been here to experience this, I would not have believed that she left so quickly and suddenly.

The nurse walked out of my Mom's bedroom and asked if she could sit at the dining room table to complete her paperwork. I said, "Yes, of course." I sat down at the table too. She said that this is such a hard thing to go through. She could call the grief counselors for me and my family. I said thank you, not tonight. We have the Chaplain coming to offer her a final prayer.

As she filled out her forms, I had to sign some of them. She asked me my Mom's time of death and I replied, "She passed at 8:00 p.m." She processed the medicines to dispose of them properly. She asked me if we had arrangements pre-planned? I said no, that this happened so fast that we didn't have time. I said she wanted to be cremated and we had researched a Mortuary that met the Better Business Bureau standards, but we had not talked to them. I told her the name of the place and she said many of her Hospice families use them. She said she would call to make arrangements to pick up my Mom's body tonight, unless we wanted to have her remain for viewing. I asked her to please call them and asked did the Coroner need to be called?

She said that because this was an expected death that the Coroner didn't need to be called. I was grateful for that. My images of someone dying came from TV and there were emergency lights and many people showing up in a chaotic commotion. I was glad it would be quiet and peaceful. She finished her paperwork and then called to arrange for Mom's body to be picked up.

She hung up the phone and said they would be here within the hour and she said she would wait with our family until they came to pick her up. I thanked her. She then told all of us that over the course of her doing this job, she had seen many people pass. Some leave and fight to their very last breath. They even have that look on their faces, but not my Mom. She said "Your Mom left in peace. You can see it on her face and that is a good thing." That was comforting to hear.

The Chaplain arrived at our house next. It was around 9:30pm when he walked into our patio. I was glad to see it was the same Chaplain who came this morning to offer prayers for my Mom. I thanked him for coming at such a late hour. He said it was no problem and that's what he is here for. He offered my family his condolences. He led us down the hallway into her room. We all gathered around and he led us in a final prayer for my Mom. I started to cry quietly. We all were crying now. When he was done we all walked into the living room and I asked him if he available to conduct services? He said he does and asked when we were thinking of doing her services. I told him next Saturday and he said he was available. He said he would be in touch with us and come out Thursday afternoon to meet with the family.

After he left I said to Auntie and Uncle that I wanted to go say goodbye to my Mom before the Mortuary came to pick her up. I walked in her room and they joined me standing in the doorway. A funny occurrence happened at that moment. As they stood by the doorway and as I walked towards my Mom, the fan that was turned on in her room made the strangest sound. As if it was whirring down, down, down. Then it went back to normal.

My Auntie and Uncle had asked each other if they had done that? They both said "No." I looked at my Mom and then at them and smiled. I said, "That was her. Mama, that's funny. It's electrical, not exactly a light flicking, but it still works". We all smiled at that. I sat next to her on the bed and put my hands onto hers. The warmth of her body was going.

I looked at her and my heart just hurt. Seeing my once beautiful, vibrant Mom, now all that remained was her frail, cancer filled body. She died peacefully. Her face had a very calm look on her face and seeing that brought my heart some comfort.

I said "Mama, I will see you one day again. We will miss you and we will be okay. Go have fun in Heaven and send me the hummingbird. Thank you for all of your love." I gave her my last kiss on her cheek and tears rolled down my face. I got up and walked to go out of her room so that my Auntie and Uncle could have their final moments with her. I went and sat on the sofa and hugged my kids. We all had a good cry.

It was getting close to 11:00 p.m. and finally the man from the Mortuary arrived in a white unmarked van. He came in our house and I showed him to my Mom's room. My Uncle went with him to see what would need to be moved so that he could place her on a gurney. My Uncle started to move items but due to the angle of my Mom's room, she would need to be carried into the hallway and be placed on the gurney.

Thankfully my Uncle had the presence of mind and said to me, "Sweetie. I need you to go upstairs. Go sit with Ron while I help my sister on the gurney. You won't want to see that." I said okay and Ron and I went upstairs and then Brittney and Michael went in his bedroom. I honestly hadn't thought about what was happening or what I would see.

My Uncle helped to carry his big sister and to place her body on the gurney. He walked outside with the man from the Mortuary, rolling the gurney with my her body outside. My Uncle is such a strong man, emotionally and physically. For him to do that final act for his big sister must have been so difficult to do. He loved her so much.

He came back in the house and called up to us and we joined everyone in the living room. The Hospice nurse gave us all a big hug and said that they will arrange to pick up all the medical items and not to worry about any of that. She reminded all of us that we had grief counseling available for up to one year after today. I thanked her and she left.

My daughter Brittney came and gave me a big hug and I hugged her back. She said she will be by tomorrow and I asked her to please drive carefully. She left to go home with her family. Uncle J came and hugged me and said he would be by tomorrow morning. I told him thank you and I was so glad he made it. He hugged everyone and left to go get some sleep. I hugged my Auntie and said I was so sorry. I thanked her for being here. I told her that I was going to go lay down. I gave Michael a hug and told him I loved him.

Ron and I went upstairs, I crawled into bed and just started crying. I couldn't stop. My husband crawled in bed to hold me and try to comfort me. I was so thankful he was holding me, but at that moment there would be no comfort. My Mom was gone and there was nothing I could do. I would have no more laughs with her, no shoe shopping, no getting scared watching our ghost shows and no more cups of coffee. I would never hear her say to me when I came home from work, "Hi Honey. How was your day?" I cried so much that night, I cried myself to sleep, as my Mom left on the final journey of dying and her soul transcended into her new spiritual journey Home.

CHAPTER 8 - THE LAST GOOD-BYE

A birth of a new life is often celebrated with joyous love. The newness of life beginning, full of promise and hope of all the possibilities life can bestow. A death is a more sorrowful event, marked with grief, loss and the finality of what can be no more. The life that was once shared has stopped with the knowing there will never be anymore words spoken, love given, holidays or special moments shared again.

The time following death is the rawest emotionally for those left behind. Grief somehow wraps its mighty arms around you and doesn't want to let go. The loss felt is a natural emotion. This is a time that family and friends will do wonders towards healing your heart. I was very lucky of the kindness and generosity that came flooding my family's way following my Mom's death.

In life, my Mom and I always gave to others and it was so comforting for people to give their love to my family now. I know Mom was smiling down on all of us to see the compassion that was bestowed for all of us. My friends and co-workers had pooled together their vacation time and gave to me a week off paid so that I could grieve and prepare for my Mom's services. I was so touched by this and words cannot thank them enough for their kindness. My neighbor and co-worker brought meals donated by other co-workers. Every night after Mom's passing, a different neighbor brought dinner over to our family and that was so touching.

On Monday morning my Uncle arrived to our house. We all had some coffee together and shared stories. My Auntie told me she was extending her time here to Sunday and that my

Uncle Glen and cousin Joel would be flying in on Friday to be here. My Uncle J said he was going to leave tomorrow, but would be back on Friday with his wife.

  The three of us were going down to make the arrangements for my Mom's cremation. I was walking out of my house with keys in hand when Auntie suggested that Uncle J drive us down. I remember saying, "I can drive. I am okay." Well, it turns out I wasn't okay. I was going through the inevitable motions of all things that are left for the families to tend to for funeral arrangements, without thinking about my emotions.

  Mom did not want a traditional burial. She did not want the pomp and circumstance of the viewing, funeral with a casket and eventual burial in the ground. For some people this is important, but not for my Mom. She wanted to be cremated. She wanted us to have a Celebration of Life service. She wanted her ashes to be split up between her children and brother and sister. She thought this way she could go travel to places with us that she didn't get to see while she was alive. She laughed and had told me she wanted to be a six pack, not like beer but a six pack of her in small urns.

  My Uncle drove us down to Mission Valley. We all shared light conversation, which I had thought I was participating in. Still, I thought to myself, *I was okay and could have drove us*. It was very nice of my Uncle to drive us down. We finally found the place, parked and walked into the building. There was another family being assisted so we all sat down and waited our turn. We walked into the office and the Director had us sit down in front of the desk. Uncle J was on my left side and Auntie M was on my right side. The Director excused himself for a moment and as he did we were looking at the assortment of urns on the shelves and I commented that I didn't like any of these and Mom wouldn't either. Auntie and Uncle agreed.

Then, the moment where my Mom's death hit me, was about to happen. The very reason my Auntie asked my Uncle to drive. The very nice Director started to discuss the different choices for my Mom's cremation and services offered. He said that I would need to fill out some forms and that is all I can remember, because after that my head and thoughts were somewhere else for a moment. I vividly remember the Director talking to me, asking questions, but I couldn't hear him! He was only a desk width away from me and I had to ask my Auntie and my Uncle what was he saying? It was a surreal moment in my life I will never forget.

I was so grateful that my Auntie and Uncle were there with me. I could not have found the strength without them there. They helped to guide me with the paperwork I had to fill out for her death certificate information and then came time for the question of my Mom's will. I had an unsigned copy of her will. She became so ill, so quickly that there literally was no time to get her will witnessed and notarized.

I cannot stress enough, as difficult as this is to face, as much as you don't want to deal with preparing a Last Will and Testament, it is crucial that this very important document be completed. I learned the hard way, because my Mom's will was not finalized, her wishes of cremation could not be rendered without majority consent of her children and an Executor could not be named to handle her affairs. Thankfully we all knew what our Mom wanted so there was no question about it.

I had to email the forms to my brother and sisters and they needed to sign and send them back with a copy of their driver's license of proof of who they were. My brother was on the road driving to San Diego, but I still sent it to him. Thankfully, I was able to talk to my sisters and they helped. It took a day to get his portion completed. Once the forms were provided to the Director, he was then able to begin the cremation for our Mom. This was a very difficult duty to handle.

Over the course of the next week there were so many details to take care of, pick a place for her Celebration of Life, place an obituary, contact friends, family, past co-workers, make her service cards, pick the music for her service, and get the luncheon squared away and get her flowers. Keep in mind, all of this had to be done in between grieving.

The hardest day was behind me now and I knew everything else would flow together. My brother arrived later that evening and it was definitely a bitter sweet reunion. My brother and I are very close, as happy that I was to see him, it was hard to be so happy *why* he was here. I was thankful he made it safely. Two of his daughters also came down with their families. It was comforting to have as much family around, however deeply missing the rest of the family that couldn't come down to San Diego.

Over the course of the next day, my home was filled with laughter as we sifted through a lifetime of photographs of our family. I pulled out all of my photo albums and my brother had packed a big box of photos that he brought down. We all took turns going through the stacks of pictures and laughing at our very wonderful family. We had all been married a couple times, and soon the laughter was asking, "Which wedding was that?" Photographs have been a wonderful favorite of mine since I was a little girl. I loved going to my Nana and Papa's house, and each visit I would pull out there photo books filled with black and white photos and look through all of the family memories of past.

After we had chosen the two-hundred plus pictures, I knew I needed to go through Mom's items to incorporate her photo memories. This was very hard to do. I didn't want to go through her things, but I needed to make sure that I represented her life with her memory boards we were going to create. A funny thing happened, when I was trying to find photos, I came across her Neil Diamond CD. We had already picked out a few songs but needed two more and there was this CD and on this album was a song called "Pretty Amazing Grace", which was fitting for my Mom. I brought the CD out with the photos I found of Mom and her trips visiting my sisters in Iowa and photos of her life when she lived out East.

We listened to the CD and decided on two songs from this. It was like Mom wanted us to find this for her. So as my brother, my children, my nieces and my Auntie and I listened to the Neil Diamond CD, we began sorting through all the wonderful memories that told a story of my Mom's colorful life. Her story of the daughter she was, the big sister, the Mom, the grandma, the Oma and the friend came alive in the photos. There were hundreds and hundreds of pictures and trying to whittle down the stacks for a good representation of her life, was a challenge.

We all took a break and all of us girls walked into her bedroom. Auntie found a stack of Mom's hats. My Mom, the diva, loved her hats, just like me. We all put one on and that's when Auntie suggested we should all wear one of her hats for her service. I then suggested that they each pick an outfit of Grandma's to go with the hat. I told the girls that Grandma would have wanted that. Through teary eyes, they all found a wonderful outfit that seemed to fit their own personalities, yet they were all of my Mom's many different, wonderful styles.

The next day I had to scan all the pictures in the computer for the video my brother's childhood friend was offering to make for us. As I scanned, and scanned and scanned, the grandchildren helped write the obituary. It was nice that everyone was helping through their own grief. We all needed to be busy, and we definitely were. My brother brought the cd of all the pictures I scanned to his friend that evening.

I was exhausted but found the strength I needed to do this for my Mom's final wishes. It took three days to work on all of the memory boards. Placing the pictures in groups of just my Mom growing up into the stunning beauty she became. A board of her and her immediate family of her parents and brother and sister and family, a board of her and her children, a board of her grandchildren and a board for Oma the great grandma.

By Thursday afternoon when the Chaplain came to meet with my Auntie, myself, my brother, my husband, my kids and nieces. These beautiful memory boards were completed. I blew up some of the most beautiful pictures of my Mom too. The Chaplain took a few minutes to view Mom's life and he said that he had never seen so many pictures for someone. We all laughed because we had hundreds more that didn't make it. I handed the picture of my Mom that I took of her when we went on a cruise to the Mexican Riviera.

I said, "This was my Mom." He commented that she was a beautiful woman and loved by her family. We all sat around and he began to ask us details of her. He asked if there were funny things she would say. We all chimed in and said "That's awesome! That's amazing!" We laughed a bit, but she would use those expressions for everything. I shared when she liked something really "girlie" she would call it "Frue Frue!"

He then asked us a profound question and that was, "What is something you would want people to know about her, what would you share?" We thought about it and started talking and we agreed that she never said anything bad about anyone. She had her challenges in life, challenges in marriage, children, but she never had an unkind word to say about someone and this was a wonderful quality of her. She was full of grace. We talked about her humor and her laugh and the wonderful warm smile she had. We would miss that. That evening after the Chaplain left, our family had dinner together and we continued sharing stories.

We had discussed if any of us were going to talk at her service and Addie said she was, I was but had no idea what I would say for fear of bursting out in tears, Auntie was going to speak about hummingbirds and the spiritual meaning they carry and Uncle John was going to talk and share his poem he wrote for his big sister.

Friday I picked up the flowers for her celebration of life services and flowers began arriving to our home. It was so sweet the love and care that was given in honor of my sweet mama. I made five beautiful arrangements with bird of paradise flowers that my Mom loved and roses. I picked up a bunch of sunflowers that Auntie and I placed inside her Bellini boots she never got to wear. We thought she would have a laugh in Heaven at that. Auntie was able to pick up her framed hummingbird pictures, from the art store. Auntie had the intention of giving these as a gift to her sister. Now they were going to be placed at the church for her service. They were lovely hummingbird pictures my Uncle Glen took at their house in St. Thomas.

I was stressing a bit on how I would say goodbye to my Mom. Over the past week I would think of things but nothing ever grabbed me to write it down. But on this Friday afternoon, I sat down and wrote my words of "On Her Spring Day". This was what I was meant to share and I would tomorrow.

Friday evening Auntie and I drove down to Lindberg Field Airport and picked up my Uncle Glen and my cousin Joel. We hugged tightly and got them loaded in the FJ. We drove back to my house and we all shared a nice dinner and lots of wine that evening. The church let us move items over for the services in the morning. I went to bed early from being emotionally exhausted. I wanted to stay up to visit, but I just didn't have the strength.

In the morning I woke up to the hustle and bustle of a full house and everyone getting ready. I grabbed a cup of coffee and a shower. I went lightly on the waterproof mascara, because I knew I would cry it off. Everyone got up and dressed for the service which was at 10:00am. All of the men went across the street to the little church and set up the video equipment and then we went over at 9:00am to get the flowers set and the memory boards placed. Auntie and I put Mom's Bellini boots filled with sunflowers on the steps leading up to the stage area in the chapel where we all would be speaking from.

      Promptly at 10:00a.m. Mom's Celebration of life services began. The beautiful picture video played with the music we picked out and the photos. We watched the story of Mom's full life through the video of pictures. It was very moving to see. The Chaplain began speaking after it completed and followed with a prayer. Then he said that the family will speak and if anyone else wanted to come up and speak they could.

My Uncle walked up and began sharing life with his big sister and then he read his Poem:

" For Mary, My Sister

I was so small.
You held my hand.

We walked down the walk,
across the big crack.

Jagged, it would trip me,
but for your hand.

You would take me,
then, to the street's edge.

I could look down the street.
The distant sea was there,
a blue line of sea and horizon.

You would hold my hand
when we walked down the dusty
unpaved alleys to the store.

I was safe, in the warm days,

when I was so small
and my big sister guided me
on the little journeys from
home to the world.

Now we are grown.
We are grown old.

The times we have lived
are different. So much
passed time and living.

I went over that far blue line,
far from the walk, your hand.

Now as we walk toward
the line between the sea
and the horizon together,

I will hold your hand,
be your small brother."

My Auntie spoke next. She shared life with her big sister and began speaking about the hummingbirds. As she spoke there were hummingbird pictures on the screen: "In modern spiritualism, the hummingbird has special meaning. Many modern beliefs describe the hummingbird as being able to intervene with the spirit world and that the hummingbird acts as a messenger. Some people believe that when they see a hummingbird, that it is a spiritual sign and can bring healing, luck, and good fortune. The hummingbird is also often associated with joy and freedom."

She went on to share what the hummingbirds have meant to our family and the visits the she has with them that Mom had with them and me too after my grandparents were gone. There is no mistaking when the hummingbird comes to visit, they fly and flutter a foot in front of your face and look right into your eyes. "It's a beautiful experience. Mary said that she would send a hummingbird."

Auntie mentioned that in honor of her sister, that all of the women in the family are each wearing a hat of Mary's and she also spoke about the boots that my Mom didn't get wear and that's why they are here filled with sunflowers she loved. That made everyone smile and laugh.

I was next to speak. Somehow I gathered my strength to stand before everyone and speak. I thanked everyone that came for my Mom's memory and her Celebration of Life. I said, "Having shared life together and a home for more than a decade together, I have been blessed. I knew it would be difficult to speak today about how wonderful she was so I wrote this poem to say goodbye.

"On Your Spring Day

The sun rose on your Spring Day.

Blue skies above, birds singing their songs.

Peace and love abound and family all around.

Gentle winds blowing, memories of your lifetime flowing.

When the sunset fell on your last Spring evening,

We gave you hugs and kisses and

whispered our last words in your ear.

Your beautiful soul found her way home

Into the gardens of Heaven,

Where flowers always bloom and

Youthful Angels dance and sing.

Your light, your love and your laughter will be missed,

Until we see you again."

    Addie, my daughter read five pages she wrote and followed with family friends that wanted to speak, did so. We ended her service with our family friend Kashious singing *Amazing Grace* for her. She loved hearing him sing, we all did, but this song was just for her. We all cried as he sang for my Mom's last song. It was very moving for him and for all of us. The service ended with a song my niece Kristin created for her Grandma Mary *"Until We Meet Again"*. It was beautiful.

    We shared a nice luncheon with everyone out in the courtyard. My dear friend Angie was there and she helped so much. I was in a numb state. I do remember Uncle Glen asked all of us women to get together for a picture of us in Mary's hats. There was Auntie Marti in the turquoise blue cowgirl hat, me in a red big brimmed hat, Brittney in a cute brown hat with an edging of leopard spots, Jessica in a big brown floppy sun hat,

Angela in a crème colored hat and Addie in a very big brimmed white with small navy stripes. We were like my Mom's flowers.

After most everyone had left the church and the men were beginning to load up things, I walked back into the chapel and played the video again of Mom, in the quietness of the chapel. Soon Auntie M joined me and my daughters. We sat there in the front row watching her life on the screen. Her flowers in the front row wearing her hats. My husband later told me that the guys all walked in to witness this special moment of goodbye.

That afternoon the family went back to my home for a gathering. We shared food and wine, love, tears and laughter. It was such an intimate gathering of family, for such a sorrowful day. As the evening dusk began to envelope the sky, we were later told by our friend and neighbor, that her and her husband we're taking their dog for a walk right around this sunset of my Mom's goodbye. Hovering all around our townhouses were the hummingbirds! So many hummingbirds! She said they had never seen so many in one place in their entire life. I was so glad she shared that with us, as it brought us all such comfort.

This experience with my Mom has been life changing for me. I miss her so very much. I want nothing more than to give her a big hug and to hear her voice again asking me "Hi honey, how was your day?". In life, however, comes death. That' a certainty. She gave to me a stronger sense of spiritualism that I thought I had lost many years ago. She gave me belief that there is more to life than that in which our physical bodies live, there is the continuation of the spiritual life.

The journey of life is a path each and every one of us are on. No one knows when their road will end or how many miles their journey will take them. The old saying of "You only have one life to live, make the most of it". That is such a true statement. Live everyday with passion. Never wait to tell your family you love them or to wait to strive for your dreams because there will be tomorrow. Tomorrow is not guaranteed. Live your life today!

My remarkable, lovely, intelligent and independent Mom, she left when she was done and she left on her own terms. She left us in her favorite season, on a very special Spring day. She left with her courage and strength. She had no unfinished business, she didn't leave in pain like the moaning ghost at the hospital or with unfinished lives, like the spirits of her favorite ghost shows. She left us in peace, in twenty-five days.

Since her passing, I have a little hummingbird that has a red neck comes to visit me often. This hummingbird was never around before and now comes to see me. She hovers a foot away from my face and looks right into my eyes. She is so close you can hear the fluttering of the wings. I have comfort in knowing it's a sign from my Mom and this makes me smile.

I have learned from her that dying is not something that should be feared anymore. We all have that fear, especially if we have not had many experiences with death. No one wants to really think about it, so the *not* knowing about death can grow into such a great fear. My Mom has given me comfort that she is in the beautiful love and light filled place that she showed me, in that last dream, when she said her last goodbye to me. You cannot take any material possessions when you pass except the most priceless one, and that is love. Love does go with you and transcends both this physical world and the spiritual one. My Mom created an empire of love during her lifetime and she left us, Marybeth, full of grace.

PROLOGUE

During the course of writing this book there were many nights I didn't feel I was emotionally up to typing away on the computer. I would go upstairs to my bedroom and lay on my bed, when the light on my closed laptop computer would turn on. I really feel it was a sign from my Mom. She did tell me she would flick the lights on and I would know it was her. We just never discussed what lights.

Blessings & Love ~ Ronda Rockwell

BIBILOGRPAHY

www.cancer.org

www.WebMD.com

www.mayclinic.org

www.sharp.com/hospice

ABOUT THE AUTHOR

Ronda Rockwell is a San Diego, Ca. native. She has raised her three children here. She epitomizes the quintessential woman, as a loving wife, doting mother and Nana. She has been an avid supporter to those in need and has been a volunteer for many great causes around Southern California. She is a multi-talented artist and business professional. She utilizes her entrepreneurial spirit and compassion in her life and for those around her. Her life experiences add a wonderful a relatable voice in her writing.

www.ingramcontent.com/pod-product-compliance
Lightning Source LLC
LaVergne TN
LVHW051602070426
835507LV00021B/2729